BUMBLEBEE

BUMBLEBEE

poems for dark times

HAYDEN VEIL

for me[1]

who provided constant support when I needed it the most, to endure that pain and agony of juggling writing, designing, editing, proof reading, publishing, whilst remaining an utter fool. At least there is nobody else to blame for this artefact

well done, you

☥

CONTENTS

FURVUS

FIGURES

PREFACE

It could perhaps be considered lunacy to even attempt writing a whole poetry collection by hand. It assumes the reader would find pleasure in deciphering the glyphs into words before searching for any deeper meaning in the written. Would a potential reader be put off by a seemingly illegible font?

This, and a variety of similar questions was solved by including two versions of each poem, the illegible and the sensible, leaving it up to the reader to decide their approach to the texts. I hope this will not diminish your experience of this collection of original poetry.

As always, I wish you a pleasant journey through the bumps and cracks of the road ahead. Thank you for reading.

HAYDEN VEIL
Cambridge, UK
March 2023

ALBIDUS

THE SWIFT

To fly beyond the red brick wall
a minor misdemeanour, the sin
of a slender swift. To fly beyond
the red brick wall

like a self's desire to flee
to escape its confinement,
the chains that stain every white sheet
every fabric of future freedoms,

carried high above the rules of men
on polished wings it found its freedom,
a swift swallow, a self proclaiming
a desire to be free

and to fly far beyond
and never to return again
to the red bricked wall
a sinner.

The Swift

To fly beyond the red brick wall
a minor misdeanour, the sin
of a slender swift. To fly beyond
the red brick wall

like a self's desire to flee
to escape its confinement,
the chains that stain every white sheet

every fabric of future freedoms,

carried high above the rules of men
on polished wings it found its freedom,
a swift swallow, a self proclaiming
a desire to be free

and to fly far beyond
and never to return again
to the red brick wall
a sinner.

HAYDEN VEIL

IN GREY HUES

Booze, too much booze
today, tonight I snooze
unwary,
unawares of every youse
in every house
dancing in grey hues
yet dreaming of a souse,
of rainbows, and a muse.

In Grey Hues

Booze, too much booze
today, tonight I snooze
unaware,
unawares of every yours
in every house
dancing in grey hues
yet dreaming of a souse,
of rainbows, and a muse.

THE MUSES' CALL TO ARMS

Not every story needs a hero.
Not every line needs to be crossed.
Not every cloud needs a silver lining.
Not every poem needs to rhyme.
Not every voice needs to be heard.
Not every sentence needs –

containment.

Not every line needs a prefix …
a choice made by those who wield the pen
casually in their hand
as they chase their missing words,
mere echoes in their unquiet minds
recalling better times
where ravens crossed the cloudless sky,
flew towards the rainbow room
and the mountain made of sand,
to find the unheard whispers –
the Muses' call to arms.

The Muses' Call to Arms

Not every story needs a hero.
Not every line needs to be crossed
Not every cloud needs a silver lining.
Not every poem needs to rhyme.
Not every voice needs to be heard.
Not every sentence needs —

containment.

Not every line needs a prefix ...
a choice made by those who weild the pen
casually in their hand
as they chase their missing words,
mere echoes in their unquiet minds
recalling better times
where ravens crossed the cloudless sky,
flew towards the rainbow room
and the mountain made of sand,
to find the unheard whispers —
the Muses' call to arms.

TIME GONE AWRY

Age is just Time on steroids,
a Meter unable to count
the lawful circumference
of fifteen point nine one
five five times
a pie too desired
to consider.

Age is just a Meter stretching,
just Time gone awry.

Time Gone Awry

Age is just Time on steroids
a Meter unable to count
the lawful circumference
of fifteen point nine one
five five times
a pie too desired
to consider.

Age is just a Meter stretching,
just Time gone awry.

Lies Intertwined

I intertwined the lies, the spoken and the heard
with lies soon unearthed.

I formed a plait, wore a short skirt
and painted lips.

I danced your night away, saw the last coil straighten
and a man slowly reverting.

I let it loose, let it fly
and left my sign.

I unpacked and embraced your final muffled words
behind the plastic mask.

I dyed it blue – my innocence
in a kiss.

I danced alone that night along the river of dreams
atop your shallow barrow.

I stopped and turned, to remember to greet
the smile of stranger with a twirl and a bow
is a lie worth pursuing.

Lies Intertwined

I intertwined the lies, the spoken and the heard
with lies soon unearthed.

I formed a plait, wore a short skirt
and painted lips.

I danced your night away, saw the last coil
straighten
and a man slowly reverting.

I let it loose, let it fly
and left my sign.

I unpacked and embraced your final muffled words
behind the plastic mask.

I dyed it blue — my innocence
in a kiss.

I danced alone that night along the river of
dreams
atop your shallow barrow.

I stopped and turned, to remember to greet
the smile of a stranger with a twirl and a bow
is a lie worth pursuing.

INCOMPREHENSIBLE

Incomprehensible: her words of love
and loving and living in a moment,
he found in there no understanding
of the magic they shared; words
so eloquently painted
on a canvas of divinity, of light
where he could only see a moment
fleeting, a lover fleeing and in love
the ultimate betrayal.

Incomprehensible

Incomprehensible: her words of love
and loving and living in a moment,
he found in there no understanding
of the magic they shared; words
so eloquently painted
on a canvas of divinity, of light
where he could only see a moment
fleeting, a lover fleeing and in love
the ultimate betrayal.

Dissection

Every book dissected,
every paragraph on every page
scrutinized,
parsed, paused and pondered
on sentence structure
on the writing in the spaces
between and below
I saw their flaws
like shooting stars in cloud-free skies,
sparkly like the diamond I parted.
I saw their flaws and failures bulging
like a tin of fermented herring;
dissected, dismembered, dismayed
I deemed them –
geniuses.

Dissection

Every book dissected,
every paragraph on every page
scrutinized,
parsed, paused, and pondered
on sentence structure
on the writing in the spaces
between and below
I saw their flaws
like shooting stars in cloud-free skies,
sparkly like the diamond I parted.
I saw their flaws and failures bulging
like a tin of fermented herring;
dissected, dismembered, dismayed
I deemed them –
geniuses.

The Letter

Wingless and chained,
your detachment shown
in the parting letter
you secretly scribbled
in my private notebook.

Rattled and rusty
I keep it close,
my attachment remains
to you and your final words

which one day, courage come!
I will read in full
to break your curse
that stuck like lovers' lips embracing,

to read in full
to summon courage,
to find another
bird of a feather.

The Letter

Wingless and chained
your detachment shown
in the parting letter
you scribbled
in my private notebook.

Rattled and rusty
I keep it close,
my attachment remains
to you and your final words

which one day, courage come!
I will read in full
to break your curse
stuck like lovers lips embracing

to read in full
to summon courage,
to find another
bird of a feather.

The Happy App

Search, search, try to find
the happy App,
the sustainable solution
to solitude.

Search, search, try to find
benevolent breadcrumbs
left by others sharing this path
from solitude.

Search, search, try to find
measurable meaning
like counting the grains
of the Sahara – blind folded.

Search, search, try to find
the happy App
selling the fictious fact
of belonging.

The Happy App

Search, search, try to find
the happy App,
the sustainable solution
to solitude.

Search, search, try to find
benevolent breadcrumbs
left by others sharing this path
from solitude.

Search, search, try to find
measureble meaning
like counting the grains
of the Sahara – blind folded.

Search, search, try to find
the happy App
selling the fictious fact
of belonging

SUMMERTIME MADNESS

In summertime the trees are full of song
And under golden rays I do belong,
Like finding once again my long-lost ball
The target now before the nightly fall
To see again her dancing down the lane
And hold her hands as lovers always do
Exuberantly,
I chase her down like many done before
But fall upon her swaying skirt a fool,
A girl no longer wanting to see me
I dream about tomorrow's trees in song.

Summertime, Madness

In summertime the trees are full of song
And under golden rays I do belong
Like finding once again my long-lost ball
The target now before the nigtly fall
To see again her dancing down the lane
And hold her hands as lovers always do
Exuberantly,
I chase her down like many done before
But fall upon her swaying skirt a fool
A girl no longer wanting to see me
I dream about tomorrow's trees in song.

HOUSE OF PAIN

Is it still there,
the green chirping world
beyond the grey window panes?

Curtains, I remember curtains
fluttering, the invisible hands
tracing lines
over checkered stripes;
I remember soiled curtains,
maybe pain of grey stains –
and a planted Dragon's Breath.

Is it still there,
the salient sign of life
beyond our creaking crumbling fences
– separating them from us?

Carpets, I remember soft carpets
slowly awakening,
becoming sentient and …
I remember soiled carpets,
magnolia, magnolia

House of Pain

Is it still there,
the green chirping world
beyond the grey window panes?

Curtains, I remember curtains
fluttering, the invisable hands
tracing lines
over checkered stripes;
I remember soiled curtains,
maybe pain of gray stains –
and a planted Drgon's Breath.

Is it still there,
the salient sign of life
beyond our creaking crumbling
                                fences
– separating them from us?

Carpets, I remember soft carpets
slowly awakening,
becoming sentient and ...
I remember soiled carpets,
magnolia, magnolia

magnolia stained by time –
and a swamp-green Shark's Tooth
in mourning.

Is it still there,
the trace of breadcrumbs,
the spell cast to summon them
paving your way into the fold.

Doors, I remember the open door,
the keys dropped
and your one-line note;
I remember vivdly
the old red door,
a closed door,
but like morning mist
my memory of you
once loved
– is fading.

magnolia stained by time —
and a swamp-green Shark's Tooth
in mourning.

Is it still there,
the trace of breadcrumbs,
the spell cast to summon them
paving your way into the fold.

Doors, I remember the open door,
the keys dropped
and your one-line note;
I remember vividly
the old red door,
a closed door,
but like morning mist
my memory of you
once loved
— is fading

MORNING COFFEE

Ah! The smell of morning coffee,
unlike her sweet and lingering perfume,
warrants exploration of another day
as the long night's memories fade.

Ah! The dripping
from dunking this stale bread,
unlike our conversations
it softens over time.

Ah! The whispers under white sheets,
like raging torrents in a pine forest dream;
and trunks made of sterner stuff than I
am.

Ah! The dreams again find their way
into the grey matter, hard as rock
to replace the traces of another.

Ah! The smell of mourning coffee.
Without it, what would I be?

Morning Coffee

Ah! The smell of morning coffee,
unlike her sweet and lingering perfume
warrants exploration of another day
as the long night's memories fade.

Ah! The dripping
from dunking this stale bread,
unlike our conversations
it softens over time.

Ah! The whispers under white sheets,
like raging torrents in a pine forrest dream,
and trunks made from sterner stuff than I
am.

Ah! The dreams again find their way
into the grey matter, hard as rock
to replace the traces of another.

Ah! The smell of mourning coffee.
Without it, what would I be?

Mirrors

Mirrors distort
essence, our perception
of self, of self …

Mirrors … turn us into another,
a not her, … a careless callous
biped seeking nothing but

but, but …
the cracks
will show

even more as shower fog descends
and her writing clears,
her essence turns sideways –

her mirror unreflecting.

Mirrors

Mirrors distort
essence, our perception
of self, of self ...

Mirrors ... turn us into another,
a not her, ... a careless callous
biped seeking nothing but

but, but ...
the cracks
will show

even more as shover fog descends
and her writing clears,
her essence turns sideways –

her mirror unreflecting.

NO CHEESE

And the man who once were a boy
woke to find a couch nibbling
on the late night crackers left
– without cheese.

And the man who once were a boy
saw a sign: EXIT, near an arrow
pointing left, the stage unlit
and no whispers.

And the man
who wished he were that boy again
found neither reassuring,
as mice hurried in the fading future
dreamt, and the man – scurried after.

No Cheese

And the man who once were a boy
woke to find a couch nibbling
on the late night crackers left
– without cheese.

And the man who once were a boy
saw a sign: EXIT, near an arrow
pointing left, the stage unlit
and no whispers.

And the man,
who wished he were that boy again
found neither reassuring,
as mice hurried in the fading future
dreamt, and the man – scurried after.

Spaces

Hidden in white spaces

a life in empty lonely lines,

beyond the full stops
where once green forests stood

like mighty pines and firs
snow-capped silver birch

no silent storms roar,
no need for more

than space, more space,

you called it space –

your freedom.

Spaces

Hidden in white spaces
a life in empty lonely lines,
beyond the full stops
where once green forests stood

like mighty pines and firs
snow-capped silver birch

no silent storms roar,
no need for more

than space, more space,
you called it space —
your freedom.

A Crime of Passion

Your golden buttercup alight,
like starlight on a dreary day,
the scene of the crime, of adventure:

I chase red ants in a blue striped suit,
slow sandy socks rest
in dusty patent leather shoes;

I crawl and trawl the murdered grass
seeking to reassert, to reestablish
dominion;

I dive and swim your blue ocean
until your grey sky becomes my dread,
my fear of drowning without escape.

Your golden buttercups
spread thinly on wholesome toast
with blacker than black Joe,

an open window and a lonely lark,
and that smile a crime of passion
– unpunishable.

A Crime of Passion

Your golden buttercup alight,
like starlight on a dreary day,
the scene of the crime, of adventure;

I chase red ants in a blue striped suit,
slow sandy socks rest
in dusty patent leather shoes;

I crawl and trawl the murdered grass
seeking to reassert, to reestablish
dominion;

I dive and swim your blue ocean
until your grey sky becomes my dread,
my fear of drowning without escape.

Your golden buttercups
spread thinly on wholesome toast
with blacker than black Joe,

an open window and a lonely lark,
and that smile a crime of passion
— unpunishable

SHAME SIMMERING

The burning, burning sensation
of failure to fully comprehend
all previously scribbled words;

Like Shame simmering on low heat
far too long, served with bread
stale like depressed air;

Cheeks on fire,
woes from weary words
turned prosaic.

Shame Simmering

The burning, burning sensation
of failure to fully comprehend
all previously written words;

Like Shame simmering on low heat
far too long, served with bread
stale like depressed air;

cheeks on fire,
woes from weary words
turned prosaic.

Shadows

You asked for a kiss, a kiss as I left,
a kiss on the cheek as I left.

You asked – I gave – leaving me wanting:
wishing more would come, more to be had,
to be needed: why yes! – needed.

You asked for a kiss so we kissed and slowly parted
like strangers we knew no more.

You asked for kiss, from me – yes me!
but I still wonder as my lips grow dry
and my thinning hair gradually greys,
as I slowly fade into your shadows:
– why, oh why did you...

Shadows

You asked for a kiss, a kiss as I left,
a kiss on the cheek as I left.

You asked — I gave — leaving me wanting:
wishing more would come, more to be had,
to be needed. Why yes! — needed.

You asked for a kiss so we kissed and
                                    slowly parted
like strangers we knew no more.

You asked for a kiss, from me — yes me!
but I still wonder as my lips grow dry
and my thinning hair gradually greys,
as I slowly fade into your shadows:
— why, oh why did you ...

SUNSHINE

Seated outside
I scroll and scroll
up and down familiar pages,
feeling nothing
but a premature birth of hay
– and fever:
the undesired twins of summer
revisiting.

The golden coat of sunshine,
tinglings on virgin skin,
burning rays of wonder
and her waving golden hair,
a growing sense of wonder:
to scroll – and to care.

There is sunshine outside,
her scrolls hidden
beyond my void,
another nothing
her birth called forth.
Attention gods!

Sunshine

Seated outside

I scroll and scroll
up and down familiar pages,
feeling nothing
but a premature birth of hay
- and fever:
the undesired twins of summer
revisiting.

The golden coat of sunshine,
tinglings on virgin skin,
burning rays of wonder
and her waving hair,
a growing sense of wonder:
to scroll - and to care.

There is sunshine outside,
her scrolls hidden
beyond my void,
another nothing
her birth called forth.
Attention gods!

Attention mortals!
Twice her lifelong longing failed
to feel my burning hands,
and I withdraw to shades calling.

There is sunshine hidden
outside life and death,
beyond our nothings
of infinite birth and death;
tumbling the gods' own hay
to awaken our feverish lust
and urge to join them
to feel their burning desire:
their rays touching us
– in a smothering sense of awe.

Attention mortals!
Twice her lifelong longing failed
to feel my burning hands,
and I withdraw to shades calling.

There is sunshine hidden
outside life and death,
beyond our nothings
of infinate birth and death,
tumbling the gods' own hay
to awaken our feverish lust
and urge to join them,
to feel their burning desire:
their rays touching us
—in a smothering sense of awe.

Blue Waves

Thoughts crest the blue waves
Foamless peaks of ecstasy
Drop and dim in hastily decent
Red bricks await

Blue Waves

Thoughts crest the blue waves
Foamless peaks of extacy
Drop and dim in hastily decent
Red bricks await

DROUGHT

Love? No. There's none left, dry
the well once sparkling, dry
the tired eye still searching, dry
the silent throat yet burning, dry
the desert of dreams: mirages
no longer skim afar,
burning bushes wither,
the whispers of night
turned cold.
Love? No, the torrent times are over,
the flower blooms
no more.

Drought

Love? No. There's none left, dry
the well once sparkling, dry
the tired eyes still searching, dry
the silent throat yet burning, dry
the desert of dreams: mirages
no longer skim afar,
burning bushes wither,
the whispers of night
turned cold.
Love? No, the torrent times are over,
the flower blooms
no more.

To Feel!

Oh, to feel again! To feel!
Punctuate the windless void
with beat from hearts, taps
from trembling hands of light,
of desire, of rage!

Oh, to feel again! To feel
something touching me
there: to punctuate the void,
a numbness animated,
a needle needs but one end!

Oh, to feel again! To feel
another's heavy heart,
another's lavish light,
coming and becoming
desire, wind, and power!

Oh, to feel again! To feel!
To punctuate the windless void!
See Desire slowly rising!
Feel a welcoming wind's embrace!
To feel! To feel! Oh, the Joy
it could bring!

To Feel!

Oh, to feel again! To feel!
Puncture the windless void
with beats from hearts, taps
from trembling hands of light,
of desire, of rage!

Oh, to feel again! To feel
something touching me
there: to puncture the void,
a numbness animated,
a needle needs but one end!

Oh, to feel again! To feel
anothers heavy heart,
another's lavish light
coming and becoming
desire, wind, and power!

Oh, to feel again! To feel.!
To puncture the windless void!
See Desire slowly rising!
Feel a welcoming winds embrace!
To feel! To feel? Oh, the joy
it would bring!

Time – The Weary Wanderer

Stars born and stars dying,
Time had seen them come and go,
no children burn as bright as those
forged in the name of fire.

How long the path of the weary wanderer,
how much further still to go,
only Time will tail they said:
malapropism with a foreign accent.

But Time wouldn't tell, couldn't
tell without hands, or legs
to stand on. Time felt abused,
left to expire,

chastised for just staying true
to the one pukka power. How long
or how much longer will Time keep
going, as silver stars align

and the world of Men obsesses –
over nothing; Time will see
stars born and stars dying,
the children of the weary wanderer
forged in the name of fire.

Time - The Weary Wanderer

Stars born and stars dying,
Time had seen them come and go.
no children burn as bright as those
forged in the name of fire.

How long the path of the weary wanderer

how much further still to go,
only Time will tail they said:
malapropism with a foreign accent.

But Time wouldn't tell, couldn't
tell without hands, or legs
to stand on. Time felt abused,
left to expire,

chasticed for just staying true
to the one pucka power. How long
or how much longer will Time keep
going, as silver stars align

and the world of Men obcesses –
over nothing; Time will see
stars born and stars dying,
the children of the weary wanderer
forged in the name of . fire.

i

i am not grown up yet,
barely reach the threshold for glyphs,
an uptight upright with a speck of dust hovering.
i am to you and You a mere minor:
an ell callously knifed but safe in survival;
a divided soul searching for home
to become as intended a freestanding character:
a moral champion for the self
without neither head nor tail:
an I – proud to be upright.

i

i am not grown up yet,
barely reach the the threshhold
                    for glyphs
an uptight upright with a speck
          of dust hovering
i am to you and You a mere minor:
an ell callously knifed but safe
              in seervival;
a divided soul searching for home
to become as intended
      a freestanding character:
a moral champion for the self
without neither head nor tail:
an I — proud to be upright.

PURPOSE TWIRLS

Through moaning mist of future days
in silent creaking shadows
Purpose twirls a mindless dance,
in search of something
a solid one thing, a break:
caught and claimed
as finders keeper;

Purpose twirls.
The cotton skirt flutters and flies
around her red raving sandals
keeping her afloat, hovering
above the safety of solid ground.

Eternity half gone, Purpose goes on
searching for someone to seduce,
for the one still searching for
the one to be claimed
by Purpose.

Purpose Twirls

Through moaning mist of future days
in silent creaking shadows
Purpose twirls a mindless dance,
in search of something
a solid one thing, a break:
caught and claimed
as finders keeper;

Purpose twirls.
The cotton skirt flutters and flies
around her red raving sandals
keeping her afloat, hovering
above the safety of solid ground.

Eternity half gone, Purpose goes on
searching for someone to seduce,
for the one still searching for
the one to be claimed
by Purpose.

A Fortune Told

Time reared its rusty scythe
towards the fortune-teller,
a fortune-told now rested
beyond the reach of existence.

Time moved on, ticking
to unwind the perpetual feathers
tickling the twinkling eyes of night
above a fallen fortune-teller.

A Fortune Told

Time reared its rusty scythe
toward the fortune-teller,
a fortune-told now rested
beyond the reach of existance.

Time moved on, ticking
to unwind the perpetual feathers
tickling the twinkling eyes of night
above a fallen fortune-teller

Meaning of Memories

A debt carried deep within, an unawareness
of place in time, a lingering doubt
this one was mine – to rule and to ravage.

I found the timeless place unfitting:
approximate and bent on breaking
all rules of rhyming, force them full
by separation: a single silent *s*
divorced from the blessed Mother.

I carry in my heart a debt,
one I never intend to forget:
you words dividing,
searching for meaning of memories
and migration: birds, beach
or the hill of Babylon;
I will never become another one.

Meaning of Memories

A debt carried deep within, an unawareness
of place in time, a lingering doubt
this one was mine — to rule and ravage.

I found the timeless place unfitting:
approximate and bent on breaking
all rules on rhyming, force them full
by separation: a single silent s
divorced from the blessed Mother.

I carry in my heart a debt,
one I never intend to forget:
your words dividing,
searching for meaning of memories
and migration: birds, beach
or the hill of Babylon;
I will never become another one

Pink Pigs Crashing

I am no poet. Wordsmiths
are a different kind of beings:
alien to my pen of blue ink;
of crumbling tapestries they weave
and conjure blue skies
from terrors deep down
where unconcerned clouds
no longer linger.

I am no poet. Writers
write their blue truths:
blue moons and pink pigs
crashing, crackling,
roasting to feed the alien men
and the beating heart
of the Lady's pen.

I am no poet. I
never saw his Skylark
soaring in his sky;
never bought her beach bird's
obsession for food, food,

Pink Pigs Crashing

I am no poet. Wordsmiths
are a different kind of beings:
alien to my pen of blue ink;
of crumbling tapestries they weave
and conjure blue skies
from terrors deep down
where unconcerned clouds
no longer linger.

I am no poet. Writers
write their blue truths;
blue moons and pink pigs
crashing, crackling,
roasting to feed the alien men
and the beating heart
of the Lady's pen.

I am no poet. I
never saw his Skylark
soaring in his sky;
never bought her beach bird's
obsession for food, food,

her Sandpiper's ceaseless search
for food; no pathos felt
for nature's deep-rooted drive
to survive.

I am no poet.
I fake, I take His words
mix and unmatch with Hers,
let slowly simmer a tepid truth
served crumb-less, cold, meatless,
untold – in a bowl for fools.

her Sandpiper's ceaseless search
for food; no pathos felt
for nature's deep-rooted drive
to survive.

I am no poet.
I fake, I take His words
mix and unmatch with Hers,
let slowly simmer a tepid truth
served crumb-less, cold, meatless,
untold – in a bowl for fools.

MEASUREMENTS

How to measure a life, compare
the time lived with the time as alive.

How do you judge that life, judge
the success without comparison
to another's, unbiased thoughts
signing the bottom line.

How do you measure a life,
a lifetime of time passing
without waves shaping any rocks
or gravel left for others.

How do you judge that life
without scale and sense,
without any signs of ever been
– alive.

Measurements

How to measure a life, compare
the time lived with the time as alive.

How do you judge that life, judge
the success without comparison
to another's, unbiased thoughts
signing the bottom line.

How do you measure a life,
a lifetime of life passing
without waves shaping any rocks
or gravel left for others.

How do you judge that life
without scale and sense,
without any signs of ever been
— alive

Morning Dew

Morning dew and fog-less dreams,
curtains drawn, mind undrawn,
dreams not yet undreamed;
a cold breeze on sticky skin,
a scream for more, more of same,
of pain from yet another day
– a painting to be finished.

Morning dew and steaming brew
awaits the silent dreamer,
the fool behind the veil
of maybes, and the sole searcher
of a lasting friendship.

Morning dew,
the bleak bleak hues
of morning fills the canvas,
becomes another maybe
in this daily search
for purpose.

Morning Dew

Morning dew and fogless dreams,
curtains drawn, mind undrawn,
dreams not yet undreamed;
a cold breeze on sticky skin,
a scream for more, more of same,
of pain from yet another day
— a painting to be finished.

Morning dew and steaming brew
awaits the silent dreamer,
the fool behind the veil
of maybes, and the sole searcher
of a lasting friendship.

Morning dew,
the bleak bleak hues
of morning fills the canvas,
becomes another maybe
in this daily search
for purpose.

Moon Pulp

I am moon pulp,
mulched memories of lament;
talking trees impart my truths,
tales of lies, of lies,
of lurid lies;

Chainsaws cry in dark nights,
my moon swoon,
I am the lucid loon:

Your Gardener in darkness,
motionless and moonlit,
the eyes of night flicker
– flirt

with memories of you, bushy
– and bloomed.

Moon Pulp

I am moon pulp,
mulched memories of lament;
talking trees import my truths,
tales of lies, of lies,
of lurid lies;

Chainsaws cry in dark nights,
my moon swoon,
I am the lucid loon:

Your Gardener in darkness,
motionless and moonlit,
the eyes of night flicker,
—flirt

with memories of you, bushy
—and bloomed.

Sunset Over Santorini

I saw the sunset over Santorini,
the desperate dying of a day
like our love destined to fade.

As I saw the sun sink beyond me
my thoughts turned to Thera:
her passion once erupted
while mine,

         oh mine,
this cold northern heart
without passion or pine

    looked upon the pairs of doves
    desperately seeking stillness
    in the setting sun of Santorini,

– will never call forth the fire.

Sunset Over Santorini

I saw the sunset over Santorini
the desperate dying of a day
like our love destined to fade.

As I saw the sun sink beyond me
my thoughts turned to Thera:
her passion once erupted
while mine,
              oh, mine,
this cold northern heart
without passion or fire

    looked upon the pairs of doves
    desperately seeking stillness
    in the setting sun of Santorini,

— will never call forth the fire.

Dreamless Foe

Breathless boredom
and chains I cannot feel;
cannot turn this wheel of fortune:
I wish I could go beyond,
break their glass ceiling:
invisible dreamless foe,
one you insist keep me Earthbound,
keep me Unfound and Unremembered;
as time moves on, ticking – tocking
I remain. I remain. I remain still
as stillness sought
by a chastised child out of breath
but bound to steaming trains
and by invisible chains
of boredom.

Dreamless Foe

Breathless boredom
and chains I cannot feel;
cannot turn this wheel of fortune:
I wish I could go beyond,
break their glass ceiling:
invisible dreamless foe,
one you insist keep me Earthbound,
keep me Unfound and Unremembered;
as time moves on, ticking — tocking
I remain. I remain. I remain still
as stillness sought
by a chastised child out of breath
but bound by steaming trains
and by invisible chains
of boredom.

Finding Elsewhere

Angels!   Angels!   Hear me!

My destiny lies elsewhere,
my lies lie far beyond these shores,
far beyond their comprehension;

Angel! Angel! Please descend!

My painted face and frozen lakes
summon no companions, shapes no future:
backwards the sight, backwards
the mind of one abandoned and obliterated
by She who wore three faces;

Angel of my prayers – hear me.
hear me and respond.
Hear me and go beyond
these shores and show me
where my destiny lies,
where I can find my answers –
or my perpetual bliss.

Finding Elsewhere

Angels! Angels! Hear me!

My destiny lies elsewhere,
my lies lie far beyond these shores,
far beyond their comprehension;

Angel! Angel! Please descend!

My painted face and frozen lakes
summon no companions, shapes
no future:
backwards the sight, backwards
the mind of one abandoned
and obliterated
by She who wore three faces;

Angel of my prayers — hear me.
Hear me and respond.
Hear me and go beyond
these shores and show me
where my destiny lies,
where I can find my answers —
or my perpetual bliss.

Kneeling Noon

Is there ever love at dusk,
as the blue moon rises
above abandoned treetops.

As dawn breaks without echoes
of birdsong once composed
in a garden forever green
by a gardener no longer loving.

As Noontime kneels and bows
to the whims of the final few
sighs of abandonment:
her love protruding;
her shadow a high tide
in moonlight.

Is there ever love
at dusk – at dawn,
or at her kneeling noon.

Kneeling Noon

Is there ever love at dusk,
as the blue moon rises
above abandoned treetops.

As dawn breaks without echoes
of birdsong once composed
in a garden forever green.
by a garener no longer loving.

As Noontime kneels and bows
to the whims of the final few
sighs of abandonment :
her love protruding;
her shadow a high tide
in moonlight.

Is there ever love
at dusk - at dawn
or at her kneeling noon

Shadow Spaces

Her desire chiselled upon his skin:
sandpiper-coloured streaks
across snow-clad clouds;
desire dancing
and bouncing along a sandy street:
grained beached treats of goldfish,
pale blue piercing eyes,
and tannoy laughter.

Her dreams like maternal mallets,
likes knives through butter-
cups and butter-
flies and beeswax sweethearts:
irresistible,
(incongruous)
escapee,
free, free, free!
– until pinioned.

Her thoughts, like bell-blue streaks
on four starless walls of solitude;
no shadows fall where shadows form –
in breathe-only
spaces.

Shadow Spaces

Her desire chiseled upon his skin:
sandpiper-coloured streaks across
snow-clad clouds;
desire dancing
and bouncing along a sandy street:
grained beached treats of goldfish
pale blue piercing eyes
and tannoy laughter.

Her dreams like maternal mallets,
like knives through butter-
cups and butter-
flies and beeswax sweethearts:
irresistable,
(Incongrous)
escapee,
free, free, free!
– until pinioned.

Her thoughs, like blue-bell streaks
on four starless walks of solitude;
no shadows fall where shadows form-
in breath-only
spaces.

Hear Me!

Hear Me! A mere echo
of a silenced speaking-voice
drowned by a roaring rage
uncaught and unrelenting.

Hear Me! A monster growl:
uttering of sweetest symphony,
veiled insanity
within –
without
mercy,
without
vengeance
in thought.

Here Me! A mere echo –
of a different time.

Hear Me!

Hear Me! A mere echo
of a silenced speaking-voice
drowned by a roaring rage
uncaught and unrelenting.

Hear Me! A monster growl:
uttering of sweetest symphony,
veiled insanity
within –
without
mercy,
without
vengeance
in thought.

Hear Me! A mere echo –
of a different time.

Keys

I played your keys, your white
temperament and your black
plasticity; the harmonies offset
by your dissonant lack of longing.

You played my keys, my pale face
of innocence and gloomy backdrop;
the harmonies offset by my lack
of personal presence.

We played each other's keys,
never in tune, never attuned,
never hearing more than
our own melodies.

Keys

I played your keys, your white
temperament and your black
plasticity; the harmonies offset
by your dissonant lack of longing.

You played my keys, my pale face
of innocense and gloomy backdrop;
the harmonies offset by my lack
of personal presence.

We played each other's keys,
never in tune, never attuned,
never hearing more than
our own melodies.

Shorts

Mother always cut my nails
short – tidy, Mother said,
always look tidy.

I always cut my nails
short – until … I said
enough now, enough!

I let my nails grow
just beyond short, still tidy
unlike Mother's fantasy child.

I let my nails grow
beyond Mother's wishes.

I let my nails grow
beyond Mother's vision.

Mother always cut my nails,
cut my spine short,
yet my umbilical cord
– is infinite.

Shorts

Mother always cut my nails
short – tidy, Mother said,
always look tidy.

I always cut my nails
short – until ... I said,
enough now, enough!

I let my nails grow
just beyond short, still tidy
unlike Mother's fantasy child.

I let my nails grow,
beyond Mother's wishes.

I let my nails grow
beyond Mother's vision.

Mother always cut my nails,
cut my spine short,
yet my umbilical cord
– is infinite.

HAYDEN VEIL

BRAGGING IN PARIS

I saw Billy Bragg in Paris
I saw Billy play guitar
I found something new not searching
on the backstreets of love.

I saw Billy strut and strum
back when innocence was young,
when every heart's desire ruled
on the grass of Champ de Mars.

I saw Billy play guitar
near our newfound Irish bar,
our Guinness tapped and shamrocked
and redhead maidens' hearts ablaze.

I saw Billy Bragg in Paris
when every daybreak was divine
our dusk always embracing
sans worries or rules.

I saw Billy Bragg in Paris.
I found something new back then,
reflections in black mirrors –
broken hearts on the Seine.

Bragging in Paris

I saw Billy Bragg in Paris
I saw Billy play guitar
I found something new not searching
on the backstreets of love.

I saw Billy strut and strum
back when innocence was young,
when every heart's desire ruled
on the grass of Champ de Mars.

I saw Billy play guitar,
near our newfound Irish bar,
our Guiness tapped and shamrocked
and redhead maidens' hearts ablaze

I saw Billy Bragg in Paris
when every daybreak was divine
our dusk always embracing
sans worries or rules.

I saw Billy Bragg in Paris.
I found something new back then,
reflections in black mirrors —
broken hearts on the Saine.

Hayden Veil

Out of Reach

Why I am yet to find the sublime:
to experience awe
instead of just endless terror;

why my wings fail to take me
higher than high, skywards
instead of death by burning;

why I doubt myself,
why trust is so abundant in others
and so lacking in a solemn self.

I ask my selves, my scattered brains,
for suggestions to resolution
for means to avoid destitution,
but only whispers gather pace:
out of bounds – out of reach.

Out of Reach

Why am I yet to find the sublime:
to experience awe
instead of just endless terror;

why my wings fail to take me
higher than high, skywards
instead of death by burning;

why I doubt myself,
why trust is so abundant in others
and so lacking in a solemn self

why I ask myself, my scattered brains
for suggestions to resolution
for means to avoid destitution,
but only whispers gather pace:
out of bounds — out of reach.

Under Amber Skies

Too many faces lost,
voices silenced under amber skies:
lost to the infinite stream
or muted by pressure,
supressed by envy
or kissed by death.

I follow too many faces,
I carry too many fading pens,
too many writing truths
while I, I never can.

Too frequently regret consumes us,
we shake and we shiver
we stop and we stare
down an abyss so dark and so dreary
we cannot but deem it our *home*.

In the home of the dark
and the home of the dreary
we find the lost faces pinned,

Under Amber Skies

Too many faces lost,
voices silenced under amber skies,
lost to the infinite stream
or muted by pressure,
silenced by envy
or kissed by death.

I follow too many faces,
I carry too many fading pens.
too many writing truths
while I, I never can.

Too frequently regret consumes us,
we shake and we shiver
we stop and we stare
down an abyss so dark and dreary
we finally deem it our home.

In the home of the dark
and the home of the dreary
we find the lost faces pinned,

and the pens piled
and the ink dried
awaiting reincarnation –
under an amber sky.

and the pens piled
and the ink dried
awaiting reincarnation —
under an amber sky.

DISINTEGRATING CELLS

Who are these disintegrating cells
disowning their purpose
in vain belief that there is grass
on the other side
of a once white picket fence,
just beyond the amber rays
of a face that knows no better
than to speak only Hercules
providing a baseline metrics
for Lotus – one – two – three
to excel in unquantifiable glory.

Who are these disintegrating cells
carrying memories of only 640kB
yet still maintaining a joy
long since lost
in the world of gigabytes
and rendered other-lands
conjured up by two-dimensional
self-proclaimed gods.

Disintegrating Cells

Who are these disintegrating cells
disowning their purpose
in vain belief that there is grass
on the other side
of a once white picket fence,
just beyond the amber rays
of a face that knows no better
than to speak only Hercules
providing a baseline metrics
for Lotus – one – two – three
to excel in unquantifiable glory.

Who are these disintegrating cells
carrying memories of only 640kB
yet still maintaining a joy
long since lost
in the world of gigabytes
and rendered other-lands
conjured up by two-dimensional
self-proclaimed gods.

R=1.5

Reality is a thin veil,
a melting sheet of ice.

I wear my skates untied,
puckered face uncovered,
a stick too short to matter,
I am forever penalised
for crossing the thin blue line
too early, too rushed
is my approach to life.

Reality is a clock expiring,
a ghastly echo of a tick
without a tock,
a tree without bark
uprooted, the storm in a cup –
overflowing; my reality
a thinly veiled matter
without presence
or point.

R = 1.5

Reality is a thin veil,
a melting sheet of ice.

I wear my skates untied,
puckered face uncovered,
a stick too short to matter,
I am forever penalised
for crossing the thin blue line
too early, too rushed
is my approach to life.

Reality is a clock expiring
a ghastly echo of a tick
without a tock,
a tree without bark
uprooted, the storm in a cup—
overflowing; my reality
a thin veiled matter
without presence
or point.

Hayden Veil

A Dance for Two

You splatter it,
the last of your blood
like oil on cheap canvas,
the tubes of dried-out paint
lie scattered along your path,
an attempt to paint a self
too out of control to care:
a mere sidekick
in the story of your life.

I walk around humming
a tune I never truly chose,
a hired extra in my own shoes,
without lines or purpose
bar filling that vacant space
in the story of myself.

We walk in circles you and I,
dancing to different tunes
in different spaces.
I know of you
but you live unawares
yet we dance, on and on
and that is all that matters

A Dance for Two

You splatter it,
the last of your blood
like oil on cheap canvas,
the tubes of dried-out paint
lie scattered along your path,
an attempt to paint a self
too out of control to care;
a mere side kick
in the story of your life.

I walk around humming
a tune I never truely chose,
a hired extra in my own shoes,
without lines or purpose
bar filling that vacant space
in the story of myself.

We walk in circles you and I,
dancing to different tunes
in different spaces.
I know of you
but you live unaware
yet we dance on and on
and that is all that matters

for now.

If we ever meet, face to face
sparks could fly and nights
become our days,
the world our private place
of play as we find ourselves
attuned to search
our destined spot
in this universe
– of us.

for now.

if we ever meet, face to face
sparks could fly and nights
become our days,
the world our private place
of play as we find ourselves
attuned to search
our destined spot
in this universe
– of us.

Becoming Poetry

How did you decide
when your writing
became poetry;

when did you dare
call yourself a poet
in light of those
that came before.

Was there a time, a moment,
a lightning strike to hit
the core; the eyes once dark
void then saw the world
without the veil:false
and fake, like trees blooming
in cold winter's night.

Was there another, like you
a dreamer, wanting to see
a world alight with powers
of the sublime, the fantastical,
and the intense interior
of the soul exposed and fragile.

Becoming Poetry

How did you decide
when your writing
became poetry;

when did you dare
call yourself a poet
in light of those
that came before.

Was there a time, a moment,
a lightning strike to hit
the core; the eyes once dark
void then saw the world
without the veil: false
and fake, like trees blooming
in cold winter's night.

Was there another, like you
a dreamer, wanting to see
a world alight with the powers
of the sublime, the fantastical,
and the intense interior
of the soul exposed and fragile.

How did you decide to continue,
when bleak dawns approached
and your words failed to manifest;
when every little thing once loved
faded, and every howling storm
brought withered leaves and tears
beyond the realms of perception.

How did you become poetry,
when all else failed.

How did you decide to continue
when bleak dawns approached
and your words failed to manifest;
when every little thing once loved
faded, and every howling storm
brought withered leaves
beyond the realms of perception.

How did you become poetry
when all else failed.

WANING MOON

I am the Child
a forever child
a waning moon
soft-skinned
silence seeker
truth speaker
without words:
a barren baron
a fortress
– abandoned.

Waning Moon

I am the child
a forever child
a waning moon
soft-skinned
silence seeker
truth speaker
without words:
a barren baron
a fortress
—abandoned.

Lights Out

Light! Oh, my precious light
where do you presently reside?
Mere mortals fail to find your face
I dream each night of a single glance.
Some say in all sincerity
you roam the tunnel of endless night.

Where! Oh, where you hide this night,
the door is lost, cannot be found,
where can I enter, where can I go
to reach your golden eye of truth.
To leave this world behind me now
I need a sign, I do need hope
to find the tunnel with one end
and walk cautiously round each bend
to find your world of light!

Lights Out

Light! Oh, my precious light
where do you presently reside?
Mere mortals fail to find your face
I dream each night of a single glance.
Some say in all sincerety
you roam the tunnels of endless night.

Where! Oh, where do you hide this night
the door is lost, cannot be found,
where can I enter, where can I go
to reach your golden eye of truth.
To leave this world behind me now
I need a sign, I do need hope
to find the tunnel with one end
and walk cautiously round each bend
to find your world of light!

ON NE PASSE PAS!

There are walls carefully crafted
over years of yearning for peace,
concrete and steel, windowless walls
deeper than their demons' lairs,
higher than the holy heavens,
thicker than the skull of ██████ ████.

Behind the walls, carefully selected
over decades of delusion: space,
silence, and a sequestered soul
searching for absolution.

Outside the walls, a world forsaken
over a lifetime of lies: time heals all

wounds.

On Ne Passe Pas!

There are walls carefully crafted
over years of yearning for peace,
concrete and steel, windowless walls
deeper than their demons' lairs,
higher than the holy heavens,
thicker than the scull of ███ ██

Behind the walls, carefully selected
over decades of delusion: space,
silence, and a sequestered soul
searching for absolution.

Outside the walls, a world forsaken
over a lifetime of lies: time heals all

wounds.

In Passing

I am the Meridian, the Guardian
of time passing, and times
standing still.

I am the Watcher, the Observer
of lives passing, and lives
finding peace.

I am the Ferryman, the Captain
of ships passing, and ships
anchored deep.

I am the Dreamer, the Catcher
of truths passing, and truths
trumped-up.

In Passing

I am the Meridian, the Guardian
of time passing, and times
standing still.

I am the Watcher, the Observer
of lives passing, and lives
finding peace.

I am the Ferryman, the Captain
of ships passing, and ships
anchored deep.

I am the Dreamer, the Catcher
of truths passing, and truths
trumped-up.

Singleton

You spoke of awakening
to search the stars for signs,

You spoke of voices calling
to answer your final ask,

You spoke of no escape
from death's dire knock,

You spoke of a future us
in your first-person voice.

Singleton

You spoke of awakening
to search the stars for signs,

You spoke of voices calling
to answer your final ask,

You spoke of no escape
from deaths dire knock,

You spoke of a future us
in your first-person voice.

Ce Soir J'écris

Writing is a journey,
onwards and upwards,
not like driving
down a cul-de-sac
unable to find reverse
or ways of turning,
getting stuck
in the weary world
of old wounds,
old truths,
old words,
and old yous.

Writing is a journey
down a new path,
a new street, a new road
in new neighbourhood,
in a new town,
a new county
or crossing borders
into new countries – but

Ce Soir J'écris

Writing is a journey,
onwards and upwards,
not like driving
down a cul-de-sac
unable to find reverse
or ways of turning
getting stuck
in the weary world
of old wounds,
old truths,
old words,
and old yous.

Writing is a journey
down a new path,
a new street, a new road
in a new neighbourhood,
in a new town,
a new county
or crossing borders
into new countries – but

always feeling cold,
always feeling lonely.

Writing
is a perpetual journey
into the unknown,
a place in time
to appreciate
rejoice and celebrate
the never-ending forging
– of you.

always feeling cold,
always feeling lonely.

Writing
is a perpetual journey
into the unknown,
a place in time
to appreciate
rejoice and celebrate
the never-ending forging
- of you.

Pie in Sky

Above the mountains high a godly sphere
The snow-capped hills and vales so deeply green,
A lush view speaks of fingers crumbling pies
Divinely minted master chef's delight,

Below dead lakes the cods sit silently
Their final bills unpaid they race away
Curtailed, with nothing left but crumbling pies
The master chef has left them all behind,

Of metaphorical pies this speaks one truth
One voice we silently abused before:
Let go, fly high, towards the sky of pies.

Pie in Sky

Above the mountains high a godly sphere
The snow-capped hills and vales so deeply
green,
A lush view speaks of fingers crumbling pies
Divinely minted master chef's delight.

Below dead lakes the cod sits silently
Their final bills unpaid they race away
Curtailed, with nothing left but
crumbling pies
The master chef has left them all behind.

Of metaphorical pies this speaks one truth
One voice we silently abused before:
Let go, fly high, towards the sky of pie.

The Hidden Poem

What's in a name, I ask, well aware
marks will be deducted by absent
quotation glyphs: Oh! the pain
of writing a life's work
in dialogue,
when no one can be bothered to read.

Like a poem hidden inside an ad
for a rundown car: tax expired
but likely to last
for another hundred thousand miles
of continuous prose.

I consider blank verse but want
at least one rhyme to stretch
across the bonnet, or boot
– either will do, as my name is

Uninspired.

The Hidden Poem

What's in a name, I ask, well aware
marks will be deducted by absent
quotation glyphs: Oh! the pain
of writing a life's work
in dialogue,
when no one can be bothered to read.

Like a poem hidden inside an ad
for a rundown car: tax expired
but likely to last
for another hundred thousand miles
of continous prose.

I consider blank verse but want
at least one rhyme to stretch
across the bonnet, or boot
— either will do, as my name is

Uninspired.

THE SWEET LIPS OF HUBRIS

I need more hubris, less restraint
to comfortably channel my God given gifts;
compare myself with the masters of blank verse,
surpass all that came before and any pretender
subsequent.

I need to shed all fears, immerse the self
in a bath of philosophical foam,
scrub my stained skin of any blemish:
seek purity and a native soul in residence
where angels fear to tread.

I need a pen, paper, and unlimited supply
of ████ *medicamentum.*

The sweet lips of Hubris

I need more hubris, less restraint
to comfortably channel my God given gifts,
compare myself with the masters of blank verse,
surpass all that came before and any pretender
subsequent.

I need to shed all fears, immerse the self
in a bath of philosophical foam,
scrub my stained skin of any blemish &
seek purity and a native soul in residence
where angels fear to tread.

I need a pen, paper, and unlimited supply
of ▓▓▓▓▓▓ medicamentum.

No Beginning, No End

It never really begun I suggest,
perhaps a child in time
I was born unwell, unfed, untrained
in all matters that matter in a world
without instructions, without guide
or printed manuals I was left to fear
all things, all times, in perpetuity.

It never really begun I suggest,
perhaps the wind took hold
of the sail she left behind,
unknowingly or unwittingly
the whiff of love long lost
was no anchor strong enough
to keep the dinghy from escaping.

It never really begun I suggest,
the child, the angry adolescent,
the man that grew out of no plant
and the old man contemplating,
are all one and the same, the same
thoughts and the same responses
to life and events best avoided.

No Beginning, No End

It never really began, I suggest,
perhaps a child in time
I was born unwell, unfed, untrained
in all matters that matter in a world
without instructions, without guide
or printed manuals I was left to fear
all things, all times, in perpetuity.

It never really begun, I suggest,
perhaps the wind took hold
of the sail she left behind,
unknowingly or unwittingly
the whiff of love long lost
was no anchor strong enough
to keep the dinghy from escaping.

It never really begun, I suggest,
the child, the angry adolescent,
the man that grew out of no plant
and the old man contemplating,
are all one and the same, the same
thoughts and the same responses
to life and events best avoided.

More or Less

You beg me to say more with less;

scant the expression
of a pervasive void,

the princess of Serendip
served chilled without a die,

succumb to echoes
of a dawntime rose awaken,

scourge to tame
the beast before you;

You beg me to say more with less
and this is it,

more or less.

More or Less

You beg me to say more with less;

scant the expression
of a pervasive void,

the princess of Serendip
served chilled without a die

succumb to echoes
of a dawntime rose awaken,

scourge to tame
the beast before you;

You beg me to say more with less
and *this* is it,

more or less.

Compare and Contrast

I compare and contrast all things,
every moment of every day I place a self
in relation to all others;
every otherwise imagined as better,
taller, thinner Life in this snowstorm
of raging rain.

I compare and contrast all words,
the attempted, the written,
some silently spoken in torrents
others howled in halcyon chambers;
all better than a self expressing
the unspoken.

I compare and contrast, and find a self
lacking.

Compare and Contrast

I compare and contrast all things,
every moment of every day I place a self
in relation to all others;
every otherwise imagined as better,
taller, thinner Life in this snowstorm
of raging rain.

I compare and contrast all words,
the attempted, the written,
some silently spoken in torrents
others howled in halcyon chambers;
all better than a self expressing
the unspoken.

I compare and contrast, and find a self
lacking.

THE THIRD DIMENSION

I overheard my words
speaking of starvation,
of their utter lack
of most vital nutrients.

I lined them up,
and spoke at length:
of metaphysical fonts,
of angles on glyphs,
and what would be
a most likely audience;
I spoke
of enjambing lines,
and they – in unison –
chanted their reply:
'*Caesura! Caesura!*'

I promised I'd try,
████████,
to place a volt

The Third Dimension

I overheard my words
speaking of starvation,
of their utter lack
of most vital nutrients.

I lined them up.
and spoke at length:
of metaphysical fonts,
of angles on glyphs,
and what would be
a most likely audience;
I spoke
of enjambing lines,
and they—in unison—
chanted their reply;
'caesura! caesura!'

I promised I'd try
~~to place a volt~~

to place a volt

amusing
as their words rolled on.

I overlaid
my maltreated words
with echoes
from times before;
let tempests howl
behind every syllable;
added distorted strings
– for the sinners.

I saw my words turn
into moshing metaphors
and slick similes;
they spoke of being
part of something sweet:
the world of song
and the supporting
– Music.

amusing
as their words rolled on.

I overlaid
my maltreated words
with echoes
from times before;
let tempests howl
behind every syllable;
added distorted strings
for the sinners.

I saw my words turn
into moshing metaphors
and slick similes;
they spoke of being
part of something sweet:
the world of song
and the supporting
⤳ Music.

BRIGHT LIGHTS

Unknown – in search for life origin:
undiscovered slivers of divinity left,
and their right to pursue a clue
in a futile mission among random stars.

Known – in search for life ending:
uncovered shades of docile truth
and the false hope of another go,
a further road that might lead us
to our final home.

Non-binary – the search for truth,
the search to escape the fools,
the truth as evidence and means
of avoidance, a searching mind
clueless yet going – ad infinitum.

Bright Lights

Unknown – in search of life origin:
undiscovered slivers of divinity left,
and their right to pursue a clue
in a futile mission among random stars.

Known – in search for life ending:
uncovered shades of docile truths
and the false hope of another go,
a further road that might lead us
to our final home.

Non-binary – the search for truth,
the search to escape the fools,
the truth as evidence and means
of avoidance, a searching mind
clueless yet going – ad infinitum.

HECATE

In starlight cold and blue behold her face,
Beside her two of guarding dogs do rest,
Of Titan birth she brings prosperity,
No wonder they built many lasting shrines,
In Thrace the worship of her grace unbound,
Her golden key to open all closed doors
That hides a smile by magic mother moon,
But can she help Demeter's offspring find,
Our Hecate across the Styx set sail,
To search until Persephone was found;
A triple goddess at our point in time.

Hecate

In starlight cold and blue behold her face,
Beside her two ol guarding dogs do rest,
Of Titan birth she brings prosperity,
No wonder they built many lasting shrines,
In Thrace the worship of her grace unbound,
Her golden key to open all closed doors
That hides a smile by magic mother moon,
But can she help Demeter's offspring feud,
Our Hecate across the Styx set sail,
To search until Persephone was found;
A tripple godess at our point in time.

The Path of the Huntress

He chose the Path of the Huntress,
a Jack with a Sleeve of Hearts,
in search for the allusive Afterlife
beyond her crumbling Cove;
in search for his missing Half
deep in the Shadowlands of Night.

He chose the Path of the Huntress,
a Jack without his Jill,
beyond the Light the Stories withered
as silence fell and voices faded.

He chose the Path of the Huntress,
a Jack without a Jill,

but searching – he is still.

The Path of the Huntress

He chose the Path of the Huntress,
a Jack with a Sleeve of Hearts,
in search for the allusive Afterlife
beyond her crumbling Cove;
in search for his missing Half
deep in the Shadowlands of Night.

He chose the Path of the Huntress
a Jack without his Jill,
beyond the Light the Stories withered
as silence fell and voices faded.

He chose the Path of the Huntress
a Jack without a Jill,

but searching — he is still.

As Dusk Sets

As dusk sets,
as twilight calls to arms
I light four candles
each night, every night
in remembrance
of brighter days
of days of snow
and icicle brows.

As dusk sets,
as innocence falls apart
I light four candles
each night, every night
in remembrance
of another life
of a life of smiles
and absent worries.

As dusk sets,
as fate charge courage
I light four candles
each night, every night
in anticipation

As Dusk Sets

As dusk sets,
as twilight calls to arms
I light four candles
each night, every night
in rememberance
of brighter days
of days of snow
and icicle brows

As dusk sets,
as innocense falls apart
I light four candles
each night, every night
in rememberance
of another life
of a life of smiles
and absent worries.

As dusk sets,
as fate charge courage
I light four candles
each night, every night
in anticipation

of a new life
of a pristine wrapping:
a shining shell on me
and with hope
– another you.

of a new life
of a pristine wrapping
a shining shell on me
and with hope
— another you

December Dove

She came loosely wrapped
in a tarpaulin waltzing,
wild fire in her hair
& bleak lips pouting,
the gentle men awaited,
seeking all her candle light,
begone the seasoned darkness,
banish now our gloomy lives.

She came loosely wrapped
on snowless ground,
ablaze as morning broke
behind a frosty night,
across a barren meadow
in the Country of Old,
the long shadows shortened
as her light faded cold.

December Dove

She came loosely wrapped
in a tarpaulin waltzing,
wild fire in her hair
& bleak lips pouting,
the gentle men awaited,
seeking all her candle light,
begone the seasoned darkness,
banish now our gloomy lives.

She came loosely wrapped
on snowless ground,
ablaze as morning broke
behind a frosty night,
across a barren meadow
in the Country of Old.
the long shadows shortened
as her light faded cold.

In Dangerous Waters

I drown, slowly sinking, I drown!
No, unawares I entered dangerous waters:
deep, deep, dark waters, troubled waters
like tears from the Goddess of Old.

Deep, deep, deep in trouble as I find
a self caught again perplexed and petrified
by a pair of eyes,
by a pair of lies I tell myself
to avoid and to escape what once was felt:
memories of yesteryears and Pompeii's final squirt
as we laid there waiting for the endless night.

I saw your eyes as I see them now,
clearly and inevitably irresistible.
I drown, then and there unable to tell
unable to convey how I fell,
how I drowned for you,
how I drowned in you,
how your tears became my undoing.

In Dangerous Waters

I drown, slowly sinking, I drown!
No, unawares I entered dangerous waters:
deep, deep, dark waters, troubled waters
like tears from the Goddess of Old.

Deep, deep, deep in trouble as I find
a self caught again perplexed and petrified
by a pair of eyes,
by a pair of lies I tell myself
to avoid and to escape what once was felt:
memories of yesteryears and Pompeii's
final squirt
as we laid there waiting for the endless
night.

I saw your eyes as I see them now,
clearly and inevitably irresistabe.
I drown, then and there unable to tell
unable to convey how I fell,
how I drowned for you,
how I drowned in you,
how your tears became my undoing.

Crowns

I wear four crowns, four rings of legacy:
two runes on right of the old world,
a single Celtic knot of the new,
and the haunting shadow of the ghost.

I wear three crowns, three countries pounding:
the old world inescapable,
the new of sinking sand,
and the all-allusive one-leafed dream.

I wear two crowns, two hopes of future suns:
a well of ink that never dries,
and parchments in abundance.

I wear my crown, a king without a castle,
crownless I bow my head
and heed the gallow's cawing.

Crowns

I wear four crowns, four rings of
                        legacy;
two runes on right of the old world,
a single Celtic knot of the new,
and the haunting shadow of the
                            ghost.

I wear three crowns, three countries
                       pounding:
the old world inescapable,
the new of sinking sand,
and the all-allusive one-leafed
                        dream.

I wear two crowns, two hopes
                 of future suns:
a well of ink that never dries
and parchments in abundance.

I wear my crown, a king
               without a castle,
crownless I bow my head
and heed the gallow's cawing.

Hayden Veil

Screend

Sometimes I find myself staring
at a screen, hoping
something will eventually move
to break the monotony of staring
at a screen.

The silence of a static screen
blaring white noise, white hope,
white sorrow
into a binary world with castles
made of sand
where only the wee hours count
towards overtime.

Sometimes I find myself staring
at a screen – just because
I can.

Screend

Sometimes I find myself staring
at a screen, hoping
something will eventually move
to break the monotony of staring
at a screen.

The silence of a static screen
blaring white noice, white hope
white sorrow
into a binary world with castles
made of sand
where only the wee hours count
towards overtime.

Sometimes I find myself staring
at a screen — just because
I can.

Unpredictable

Unpredictable world:
unpredictable words,
the flow of fickle letters –
trickling or raging storms;
unpredictable words,
written but unpublished –
unconsidered yet shared,
regretted but too deeply nailed:
crucified upon a polished pine
surface.

Unpredictable world:
unpredictable words,
the voice of the silent man –
tongue tied and tired;
unpredictable words,
wanting but undesirable –
unspoken yet longed for,
ravaged dystopian dream:
corsets and neckties
spinning.

Unpredictable world:

Unpredictable

Unpredictable world:
unpredictable words,
the flow of fickle letters –
trickling or raging storms;
unpredictable words,
written but unpublished –
unconsidered yet shared,
regretted but too deeply nailed:
crucified upon a polished pine
surface.

Unpredictable world:
unpredictable words,
the voice of the silent man –
tongue-tied and tired,
unpredictable words,
wanting but undesirable –
unspoken yet longed for,
ravaged dystopian dream:
corsets and neckties
spinning.

Unpredictable world:

unpredictable words,
unspoken truths
in hiding.

upredictable words,
unspoken truths
in hiding.

A TWO-ACT PLAY

You analysed me

like an English literature text,

searching for the cause and effect

in your sinister two-act play:

the maiden in distress

turned weary wicked witch;

your wanton ways with

nothing to display.

I did fall, but not for your thin veil

(of insecurity), no I fell

for the lovely lass that turned

down a one-way street.

A Two-act Play

You analysed me
like an English litterature text
searching for the cause and effect
in your sinister two-act play:
the maiden in distress
turned weary wicked witch;
your wanton ways with
nothing to display.
I did fall, but not for your thin veil
(of insecurity), no I fell
for the lovely lass that turned
down a one-way street.

Streams

Streams
trickled down bushy boulders
in the sunshine
of an early spring.

Streams
now freezing up
with crystals forming
on every creaking branch.

Streams
like sunshine, will return
later as darkness lifts
over paralysed worlds,
worlds in mourning,
worlds in pain,
the tears now hard as ice will melt,
again trickle down bushy boulders,
no longer wait to unfreeze
a life of flowing.

Streams

Streams
trickled down bushy boulders
in the sunshine
of an early spring.

Streams
now freezing up
with crystals forming
on every creaking branch.

Streams
like sunshine, will return
later as darkness lifts
over paralysed worlds,
worlds in mourning,
worlds in pain,
the tears now hard as ice will melt,
again trickle down bushy boulders,
no longer wait to unfreeze
a life of flowing.

HAYDEN VEIL

YOU NEED TO EAT MORE POETRY

uncooked, the virgin shape,
sustenance for wandering souls
hiding in shadows cast by the moon,

void the light the darkness craves,

a sacrificing hand
on each page
as the moon needs
crying eyes
to wax

the poet
setting words
alight

You Need to Eat More Poetry

uncooked the virgin shape,
sustenance for wandering souls
hiding in shadows cast by the moon,

void the light the darkness craves,

a sacrificing hand
on each page
as the moon needs
crying eyes
to wax

the poet
setting words
alight

LITTLE WHITE LIES

With seasons passing
more frequent than before,
colour blindness creeping in
when judgement calls are done,
well defined truths
no longer stands the moral high ground,
the scrutinising committee bypassed
time after time,
the pockets filled with cover-ups,
a tippex rarely used,
two cans of white spray paint –
gloss and matt up my sleeves
but worst of all the filter
I keep inside my head:
only letting out the truths
I am prepared to face.

little white Lies

With seasons passing
more frequent than before,
colour blindness creeping in
when judgement calls are done,
well defined truths
no longer stands the moral high
ground.
the scrutinising committe bypassed
time after time,
the pockets filled with cover-ups,
a tipper rarely used,
two cans of white spray paint –
gloss and matt up my sleeves
but worst of all the filter
I keep inside my head:
only letting out the truths
I am prepared to face.

CANESCENS

CAGED

Caged, stainless gleaming steel
and one creaking gate left open,
unguarded

the silent moan of another ghost
left wanting,
left

wanting, wishing to dye
the pale bones
of the merry Makers,

the troubled Takers
of a life given,
unawares

the youth led astray
to become a man
in their hollow image

would lock the cage
without a key, eyes shut
– and moaning.

Caged

Caged, stainless gleaming steel
and one creaking gate left open,
unguarded

the silent moan of another ghost
left wanting,
left

wanting, wishing to dye
the pale bones
of the merry Makers,

the troubled Takers
of a life given,
unawares

the youth led astray
to become a man
in their hollow image

would lock the cage
without a key, eyes shut
— and moaning.

MUTED MOON

Embedded in the muted Moon
curved claws spurned the crumbs,
my bones
my shadow
my longing for another
demanded the sacrifice
of a soul: my soul
my own goal
and the voice
turned silent.

New Moon, never noon
no crumbs left
to follow; I caved
I . . . gave
no crumbs
no crumbs
no way to find

Muted Moon

Embedded in the muted Moon
curved claws spurned the crumbs,
my bones
my shadow
my longing for another
demanded the sacrifice
of a soul; my soul
my own goal
and the voice
turned silent.

New Moon, never noon
no crumbs left
to follow; I caved
I ... gave
no crumbs
no crumbs
no way to find

me. Me and my voice
sacrificed.
Spurned.
Silenced.
Scorned like corn
kissed by Fusarium Verticillioides
on the night of a muted Moon

rising, and a voice silenced
on a rattling heap of bones
behind the shadow of a soul
– longing.

me. Me and my voice
sacrified.
Spurned.
Silenced.
Scorned like corn
kissed by Fusarium Verticillioides
on the night of a muted Moon

rising, and a voice silenced
on a rattling heap of bones
behind a shadow of a soul
— longing

Eve

I saw the three faces of Eve
and bleaker days came and went,
through lingering smoke
a blue China cup, and memories
like an old TV set
the white and the black
dreams came and went.

I saw the three faces of Eve
hoping, dreaming, wishing selfishly
for replacement faces
for other places
to leave more traces
for you to find; a bleaker face
watched her turn
into one.

I saw the three faces of Eve
wishing
for more
than one.

Eve

I saw the three faces of Eve
and bleaker days came and went,
through lingering smoke
a blue China cup, and memories
like an old TV set
the white and the black
dreams came and went.

I saw the three faces of Eve
hoping, dreaming, wishing selfishly
for replacement faces
for other places
to leave more traces
for you to find; a bleaker face
watched her turn into one.

I saw the three faces of Eve
wishing
for more
than one.

Beans on Toast

I'm baked beans
looking for toast,
an old lover's tape
silenced; remember
those tapping sounds
across your heaving chest.

I am cold baked beans,
a stream of dreams
beyond the fears
of finding the player
broken;
I'm broken,
a mere token
of withering skin
and soundless whispers
wishing you home
where the fingers
once did the talking.

Beans on Toast

I'm baked beans
looking for toast,
an old lover's tape
silenced; remember
those tapping sounds
across your heaving chest.

I am cold baked beans,
a stream of dreams
beyond the fears
of finding the player
broken;
I'm broken,
a mere token
of withering skin
and soundless whispers
wishing you home
where the fingers
once did the talking.

HAYDEN VEIL

I'm baked beans

{looking for toast}

in a tin – shelved
and forgotten.

I'm baked beans
        {looking for toast}
in a tin — shelved
and forgotten.

NO STRANGER

My future is no stranger,
it is the mirrorless face
of sameness, sadness
dancing between blackened trees
burnt to the ground by passions
for someone,   something
now elusive.

My future is no stranger,
Hello Faceless Demon! I see your bet
and raise you all I possess
then race you till the end
of time, searching for other kind
of mirror.

My future is no stranger,
it is that which always has been
and that which always will continue to be
seen in the cause without effect –
in the mirror sighing.

No Stranger

My future is no stranger,
it is the mirrorless face
of sameness, sadness
dancing between blackened trees
burnt to the ground by passions
for someone,   something
now elusive.

My future is no stranger
Hello Faceless Demon! I see your bet
and raise you all I possess
then race you till the end
of time, searching for another kind
of mirror.

My future is no stranger,
it is that which always has been
and that which always will
                        continue to be
seen in the cause without effect —
in the mirror sighing.

Words vs. Poetry

Sometimes words become poetry,
but most times they disintegrate
into glyphs, wasted ink
on wasted trees, wasted bark
becoming pulp – fiction.

Sometimes words – are
just that, words; and you
wouldn't know the difference
if it hit you in the head
like a hammer on a rusty spike.

You wouldn't see my words
as I talk to you about matters
most urgent!

!!!!

I'm talking to you,

Dimwit,

Darned witch.

Sometimes words become poetry,
but most of the time
– not.

Words vs. Poetry

Sometimes words become poetry
but most times they disintegrate
into glyps, wasted ink
on wasted trees, wostd bark
becoming pulp — fiction
Sometimes words — are
just that, words; and you
wouldn't know the difference
if it hit you on the head
like a hammer on a rusty spike.

You wouldn't see my words
as I talk to you about matters
most urgent!

!!!!

I'm talking to you,
Dimwit,
Damned witch.
Sometimes words became poetry
but most of the time
— not.

Creaking

creaking in a blessed night,
wickerwork and cold shower
taps; they made another,
an other spawned from darkness
of night – and of minds
creaking.

Creaking

creaking in a blessed night
wickerwork and cold shower
taps; they made another,
an other spawned from darkness
of night – and of minds
creaking

Hayden Veil

Facets of an Unpolished Rock

No one shares him, no one will
carry forth his stories: the facets
of an unpolished rock
slowly disappearing
slowly becoming a desert
– devoid of mirages.

Facets of an Unpolished Rock

No one shares him, no one will
carry forth his stories: the facet
of an unpolished rock
slowly disappearing
slowly becoming a desert
– devoid of mirages.

Lust for Life

No steaming Calzone,
no empty calories
can sustain my starving souls.

No lingering smoke,
no uncaught coughs
can dim my vacant sights.

No white pellets,
no seasonal sanity
can sway my straying corpses.

No back-alley bright enough,
no seductive sea calm enough
to rediscover my lust for life.

Unsung, my song of hope:
feed me, find me, free me
from these grey demons' control,

and rekindle my eternal fire –
once more.

Lust for Life

No steaming Calzone,
no empty calories
can sustain my starving souls.

No lingering smoke,
no uncaught coughs
can dim my vacant sights.

No white pellets,
no seasonal sanity
can sway my straying corpses.

No back-alley bright enough,
no seductive sea calm enough
to rediscover my lust for life.

Unsung, my song of hope:
feed me, find me, free me
from these grey demons' control,

and rekindle my eternal fire —
once more.

HAYDEN VEIL

THE SHADOW OF THE TAIL

Away – my only direction is away,
far far away from this, from now,
from everything before the next fall,
the next rise to pursue the shadow
of the tail, to get away
from a self – in constant pursuit.

The Shadow of the Tail

Away – my only direction is away
far far away from this, from now,
from everything before the next fall,
the next rise to pursue the shadow
of the tail, to get away
from a self – in constant pursuit.

THE KLOCK & THE KLOWN

The old creaking rocking chair,
like your silent childhood clown
would never stop swaying,
never stop squeaking,

never become more than
another trusted old friend
the unwound grandfather clock
would abandon,

as the child sought answers
where no bottles were allowed,
where no pipes would remain unclean
for long,

and so the child sought and searched
in every cranny and in every nook
in every port of creation
only to find a wailing wooden horse

with a drunk clown upon it,
desperate to alight and find comfort
in the billowing smoke as the sea swelled
and the child soaked

in the one remaining bottle left open.

The Klock & the Klown

The old creaking rocking chair,
like your silent childhood clown
would never stop swaying,
never stop squeaking,

never become more than
another trusted old friend
the unwound grandfather clock
would abandon,

as the child sought answers
where no bottles were allowed,
where no pipes would remain unclean
for long,

and so the child sought and searched
in every cranny and in every nook
in every port of creation
only to find a wailing wooden horse

with a drunk clown upon it,
desparate to alight and find comfort
in the billowing smoke as the sea swelled
and the child soaked
in the one remaining bottle left open.

And the Bell Tolled

It's half past the long road
it's a quarter to cremation
and the longer I remain here
the further away I float,

with my eyes wide open
my beck becomes a river,
white and purging my scarred skin
from every trace of a lucid life,

and the river becomes a lake
and the lake becomes the sea,
and freshwater fish turn salty
in this my new reality,

where the quarter-to bell tolls
approaching cremation,
nearing the end of the infinite road
leading to somewhere, anywhere –
will do.

And the Bell Tolled

It's half past the long road,
its a quarter to cremation
and the longer I remain here
the further away I float,

with my eyes wide open
my beck becomes a river,
white and purging my scarred skin
from every trace of a lurid life,

and the river becomes a lake
and the lake becomes the sea,
and freshwater fish turn salty
in this my new reality,

where the quarter-to bell tolls
approaching cremation,
nearing the end of the infinite road
leading to somewhere, anywhere –
will do.

Snakes

Green leaves and creaking branches,
in my jungle something tempting moves,
a howl, a whisper, a rainbow's call,

I fry my madness in lard,
charred pieces await you,
yummy yummy you,

I toast my sorrow over virgin fire,
sprinkle thinly on melting ice cream,
sweet sweet betrayal,

I down my final pint, drown on dry land,
my cheers and two-finger salute
greet no one, gulp gulp bittersweet,

I await a stir, a moment of hurt
deep enough to crack the shell,
enough to greet, to mourn,

I wait, but in nature nothing moves,
in my jungle of withering leaves
nothing moves – but snakes.

Snakes

Green leaves and creaking branches,
in my jungle something tempting moves,
a howl, a whisper, a rainbow's call,

I fry my madness in lard,
charred pieces await you,
yummy yummy you,

I toast my sorrow over virgin fire,
sprinkle thinly on melting ice cream,
sweet sweet betrayal,

I down my final pint, drown on dry land,
my cheers and two finger salute
greet no one, gulp gulp bittersweet,

I await a stir, a moment of hurt
deep enough to crack the shell,
enough to greet, to mourn.

I wait, but in nature nothing moves,
in my jungle of withering leaves
nothing moves – but snakes.

No Longer in Circulation

Her time was circular, returning once
every day, every week, every ...
every bleeding hopeless dream

in agony. Never free, never free
from her crimson curse. Like
stickers slowly stuck on to trace

her youthful years; another year
another calendar, another slow
forced feature of her cultural heritage;

another calendar empty until not,
and so her power grew, to wobble
then wilt, to scream and shout

until the deaf no longer cared a whit.
She said as much to me, but I –
I only remember her first bleed.

Her time was circular, returning once
every day, every week the same
monotonous speak, a wall

No Longer in Circulation

Her time was circular, returning once
every day, every week, every ...
every bleeding hopeless dream

in agony. Never free, never free
from her crimson curse. Like
stickers slowly stuck on to trace

her youthful years; another year
another calendar, another slow
forced feature of her cultural heritage

another calendar empty until not,
and so her power grew, to wobble
then wilt, to scream and shout

until the deaf no longer cared a whit.
She said as much to me, but I —
I only remember her first bleed.

Her time was circular, returning once
every day, every week the same
monotonous speak, a wall

of silence, peering eyes unmet
and the timid times
around gathered wood:

the circular table of taciturnity,
food fed to pigs in blankets
but snorting silenced

by wordless stares; worthless care
shaped her, men in white coats
caught her and flashing lights,

the red and the black, brought her
to needles: away away
please let me stay,

I remember her say.

Her time was circular, returning once
every day to the same place,
the same space,

of needless suffering, facing only
herself: reflections in a round mirror,
split hair and pale nails my lasting memory

of her.

of silence, peering eyes unmet
and the timid times
around gathered wood:

the circular table of taciturnity,
food fed to pigs in blankets
but snorting silenced

by wordless stares; worthless care
shaped her, men in white coats
caught her and flashing lights.

the red and the black, brought her
to needles: away away
please let me stay,

I remember her say,

Her time was circular, returning once
every day to the same place,
the same space.

of needless suffering, facing only
herself: reflections in a round mirror
split hair and pale nails my lasting memory
of her.

Teddy

Teddy did not move
,   but there was room:
no   physical constraints
&
no   clattering chains;

Please move I said, your basin
is dry
now,   the demons gone
and I have this towel
to dry your weary eye
s,

– lakes never swim the poster claim
, but Teddy remain   s
in stasis: soaked   yet
          dry; his eye

prostituted   like
the dove I fried   for breakfast;

Teddy did not see my chain
placed upon his furry skin

Teddy did not move
,   ever   again

.

Teddy

Teddy
did not
move
but there
was room
on
physical
constraints
& no clothing
chains;

please move
I said,
your basin
is dry
now
the demons
are gone
and I have
this towel
to dry
your weary
eye
?

~ lake never
swim
the poster
claim
, but Teddy
remain
in stasis;
soaked yet
dry; his eye
prostituted
like the dove
I tried
for breakfast

Teddy did not
see my chain
placed upon
his torn skin

Teddy did not
move
, ever again.

Empty Space

I cannot wait for Madness to strike,
for Her holy high to arrive,
to come and embrace this vacant space
so carefully composed.

I wait for Madness in every shape,
shapeless whispers of Her faith
like a doom bell keeps me awake
at night, at noon the death knell calls
for every single soul.

I contemplate my solid position:
the bottom rung reserved,
my kind abandoned and unappreciated
in their world of permanent insanity.

I embrace Her gentle touch,
whisper my desire to escape
this lonely space, to climb
the ladder towards permanency,
to fulfil what She set out.

Empty Space

I cannot wait for Madness to strike,
for Her holy high to arrive,
to come and embrace this vacant space
so carefully composed.

I wait for Madness in every shape,
shapeless whispers of Her faith
like a doom bell keeps me awake
at night, at noon the death knell calls
for every single soul.

I contemplate my solid position:
the bottom rung reserved,
my kind abandoned and unappreciated,
in their world of permanent insanity

I embrace Her gentle touch,
whisper my desire to escape
this lonely space, to climb
the ladder towards permanency,
to fulfill what She set out.

Miss a Miss

A dishwasher for the soul,
I miss a dishwasher for the soul,
maybe a washer-dryer would do
to cleanse and clean
to scrub and scour
the dreary dreams and dark demons;
to start afresh, the smell of roses
purged and missed no longer:

.

Miss a Miss

A dishwasher for the soul.
I miss a dishwasher for the soul,
maybe a washer-dryer would do
to cleanse and clean
to scrub and scour
the dreary dreams and dark demons;
to start afresh, the smell of roses
purged and missed no longer.

Pastrami on Toast

I slice your insincerity like pastrami
to cover my buttered toast;
the orange juice, the fresh brew
left untouched.

I grate your cheese, lactose-free
lies upon lies upon piles piled
beyond our safe zone; fake phones
and purged porn drape our doors.

I toss the remnants of every us
down the revolving drain;
not recycling our dead dreams
of an inconceivable infinity.

I slice my last days into slivers
of meaning, glyphs into characters
forming words of wonderment
equally spaced into sentences,
purposely punctuated
into paragraphs of paranoia;
I keep on digging deep
the hole of my final escape.

Pastrami on Toast

I slice your insincerity like pastrami
to cover my buttered toast;
the orange juice, the fresh brew
left untouched.

I grate your cheese, lactose-free
lies upon lies upon piles piled
beyond our safe zone; fake phones
and purged porn drape our doors.

I toss the remnants of every us
down the revolving drain;
not recycling our dead dreams
of an unconceivable infinity.

I slice my last days into slivers
of meaning, glyphs into characters
forming words of wonderment
equally spaced into sentences,
purposely punctuated
into paragraphs of paranoia;
I keep digging deep
the hole of my final escape.

The Caretaker

I am the caretaker of a soul.

Shards of a life echo from dusk till dawn,
reverberates as the sun rises
fades in its dying light;

and so I care,
and care for an echo of a distant past
through eyes of icy innocence
and devoid – of all hope.

I am the caretaker of a soul
– fading.

The Caretaker

I am the caretaker of a soul.

Shards of a life echo from dusk till dawn,
reverberates as the sun rises
fades in its dying light;

and so I care,
and care for an echo of a distant past
trough eyes of icy innocense
and devoid – of all hope.

I am the caretaker of a soul
– fading

In Tempest Dawn

Thoughts flickering like candles
in tempest dawn, monsoon morning
rising stiffly.

Prescription pills
and thoughts flickering,
running down empty lanes of lunacy;
searching? unfounded lies listening?
silence, as long as silence…
there is peace!
silent mysteries? & thoughts
listening. Shhhhhh!

I light another pipe,
another nocturnal pondering
on the unwavering winds of change,
and on thoughts – flickering.

In Tempest Dawn

Thoughts flickering like candles
in tempest dawn, monsoon morning
rising stiffly.

Prescription pills
and thoughts flickering,
running down empty lanes of lunacy;
searching? unfound lies listening?
silence, as long as silence ...
there is peace !
silent mysteries? & thoughts
listening. Shhhhhh!

I light another pipe,
another nocturnal pondering
on the unwavering winds of change,
and on thoughts — flickering.

Jelly

You wrote about jelly-
fish, and I fell back into our pond
of memories, of 5am rowing out
across the silent lake
through the haze
of last night's howling moon,

and the empty bottles
and the screams
and my hiding
and the tears
and the sorries.

You wrote about jellyfish
but I drowned
beneath their nets,
suffocated
by their ignorance.

You wrote about jellyfish
and I fell back into my pond
of blancmange
and raspberries.

Jelly

You wrote about jelly-
fish, and I fell back into our pond
of memories, of 5am rowing out
across the silent lake
through the haze
of last night's howling moon,

and the empty bottles
and the screams
and my hiding
and the tears
and the sorries.

You wrote about jellyfish
and I fell back into my pond
of blancmange
and raspberries.

Lost Footing

Death became our chorus,
a backdrop with faded lights,
the wind that drove the leaf insane
in search for safer havens.

Death became our comfort blanket,
stories in times of daze.
The whirlpool to drown our hope
short of everlasting peace.

Death became our causality,
a backdoor ajar,
the spilled ink on our pale skin
awaiting a truer purpose.

Death became our hymn,
a few mumbled words,
the fake truth
inevitable.

Death became our life,
a few steps at a time,
the lost footing
incongruous.

Lost Footing

Death became our chorus
a backdrop with faded lights,
the wind that drove the leaf insane
in search for safer havens.

Death became our comfort blanket,
stories in times of daze.
The whirlpool to drown our hope
short of everlasting peace

Death became our causality,
a backdoor ajar,
the spilled ink on our pale skin
awaiting a truer purpose.

Death became our hymn,
a few mumbled words,
the fake truth
inevitable.

Death became our life
a few steps at a time,
the lost footing — incongruous.

Shooting Star

We played a game doomed to fail
on a checkered board
with only black pieces.

We danced round a Christmas tree:
abandoned angels and fading star
with needles caught
on cotton socks.

We left the blueberry pie to dry,
to crack and to crumble
in a bitter winter's night.

We gave it a shot:
I shut down
as you shot up
becoming the star
in your own darkening Universe.

Shooting Star

We played a game doomed to fail
on a checkered board
with only black pieces.

We danced around a Christmas tree:
abandoned angels and fading star
with needels caught
on cotton socks.

We left the blueberry pie to dry,
to crack and to crumble
in a bitter winter's night

We gave it a shot:
I shut down
as you shot up
becoming the star
in your own darkening Universe.

Hayden Veil

A Life in D-Minor

A single string vibrating,
a cordless agony in D-minor;
I stand, I flail; I flop, I wail;
no, not again and never more,

I will make my stand:
take my hand and pull me in,
pull me hard towards your light,
away from this perpetual night –
across northern moors at midnight:
we run we roam, free as birds
in early spring, like children
without constraints – unshackled
and full of dreams;
our moon rests on the summit.

A single string slowly pulling
our dreams into another place,

A Life in D-Minor

A single string vibrating
a cordless agony in D-minor,
I stand, I flail; I flop, I wail;
no, not again and never more,

I will make a stand:
take my hand and pull me in,
pull me hard towards your light,
away from this perpetual night —
across northern moors at midnight:
we run and we roam, free as birds
in early spring, like children
without constraints — unshackled
and full of dreams;
our moon rests on the summit.

A single string slowly pulling
our dreams into another place

worldly vibrations
of a carrier pigeon
and the song of one
becomes a lasting memory,
our terminal thoughts
accompanied by strings playing
in consonance our final tune:
our goodbyes – in D-minor.

worldly vibrations
of a carrier pidgeon
and the song of one
becomes a lasting memory,
our terminal thoughts
accompanied by strings playing
in consonance our final tune:
our goodbyes – in D-minor.

Masochistic Mayhem

There should be tears,
there should be shouts
of fear and toys thrown
from prams, and jealousy.

There should be fears,
there in the rocking chair
of horror and boys grown
from toddlers, and rage.

There should be horrors,
there behind a truth untold
of suffering and silent posts
in parenthood, and pain.

There should be suffering,
there on the naughty step
of old and the reopened
wounds, and the new.

Masochistic Mayhem

There should be tears,
there should be shouts
of fear and toys thrown
from prams, and jealously.

There should be fears,
there in the rocking chair
of horror and boys grown
from toddlers, and rage.

There should be horrors,
there behind a truth untold
of suffering and silent posts
in parenthood, and pain.

There should be suffering,
there on the naughty step
of old and the reopened
wounds, and the new.

Hayden Veil

After the Fall

White eyes searching
an abandoned sky,
powdered snow
and a bleeding nose,
white coats rejecting
your ceiling strolls,
powdered pills prescribed
as solidified Hell,

with pretence
on the canvas
we paint every day
in solid light hues,
darkness moves
in the brightest of light,
invisible selves roam
in circles of eight,

behind closed curtains
you sit and watch

After the Fall

White eyes searching
an abandoned sky
powdered snow
and a bleeding nose,
white coats rejecting
your ceiling strolls,
powdered pills prescribed
as solidified Hell,

with pretence
on the canvas
we paint every day
in solid light hues,
darkness moves
in the brightst of light,
invisible selves roam
in circles of eight,

behind closed curtains
you sit and watch

the world spinning
out of control,
your white eyes searching
for a sunlit sky
with powdered winter snow,
naked
and undiagnosed.

the world spinning
out of control,
your white eyes searching
for a sunlit sky
with powdered winter snow,
naked
and undiagnosed.

A&E

My coat of sorrow,
the reflected echo
of a rusty spade
beside the hole
I kept digging.

I never summoned rain,
never left any hope
of ever finding doors,
an escape into the world
of *normal*,

into your world
where A follows B
and lights only come on
when buttons are pressed.

Dangling from above:
that hole is not a hole,
I would not call
that spade a spade,
the lights are off
and no buttons to press,

A&E

My coat of sorrow,
the reflected echo
of a rusty spade
beside the hole
I kept digging.
I never summoned the rain,
never left any hope
of ever finding doors,
an escape out into the world
of normal,

into a world
where A follows B
and lights only come on
when buttons are pressed.

Dangling from above:
that hole is not a hole,
I would not call
that spade a spade,
the lights are off
and no buttons to press,

the whole alphabet
is dancing merrily
around a tree
except A follows E,
and there are no tears
to shed.

the whole alphabet
is dancing merrily
around a tree
except A follows E
and there are no tears
to shed.

A Dream in Three Acts

Three hours? Three hours! Three hours of hell,
then three blinks and Death enters:
pokes, asks, pokes again, asks then
if I am ready to play. I wheeze,
caught tongue-tied in the driest of deserts,
petrified to play the game of one final hour;

I seek a safer haven, a shelter from the stirring storm,
to lighten my load as escape will unfold. I wheeze,
tongue tied to the tree of life
as bark meet virgin lips in a silent lullaby,
I dream of dust and barren beaches
hear a raven's call – the summons to the final feast;

Then a poke, and another
lifts the lids too tired to fathom and fear
the burning apparition floating up ahead.
I pray as I crawl closer and closer:
be real, be real, you cheaply cut outline
of a figure, like the last mannequin
in a closed-down store waiting in anticipation
for anyone to call – only to find it gone,

A Dream in Three Acts

Three hours? Three hours! Three hours of hell,
then three blinks and Death enters:
pokes, asks, pokes again, asks then
if I am ready to play. I wheeze,
caught tongue-tied in the driest of deserts,
petrified to play the game of one final hour;

I seek a safer haven, a shelter from the stirring storm
to lighten my load as escape will unfold. I wheeze,
tongue-tied to the tree of life
as bark meet virgin lips in a silent lullaby,
I dream of dust and barren beaches
hear a raven's call—the summons to the final
                                    fiest;

Then a poke, and another
lifts the lids too tired to fathom or fear
the burning apparition floating up ahead.
I pray as I crawl closer and closer:
be real, be real, you cheaply cut outline
of a figure, like the last mannequin
in a closed-down store waiting in anticipation
for anyone to call — only to find it gone,

the salvation, solution to the simple unthought truth
of moisture, of tears, or rain to reawaken
for real this time the tongue-tied tired mind
of the dreamer.

the salvation, solution to the simple unthought
truth
of moisture, of tears, or rain to reawaken
for real this time the tongue-tied tired mind
of the dreamer.

Dusty Roads

Intemperate the soul that walks your skin
along blocked meridians, along the remnants
of a stagnant life once lived;

Eager the infant child to walk anew
the same paths unforgotten;

Intemperate the souls that roam
the eternal roads in search of other victims,
of other beasts to tame;

Eager infant children walk anew
the dusty roads unending.

Dusty Roads

Intemparate the soul that walks your skin
along blocked meridians, along the remnants
of a stagnant life once lived;

Eager the infant child to walk anew
the same path unforgotten;

Intemperate the souls that roam
the eternal roads in search of other victims,
of other beasts to tame;

Eager infant children walk anew
the dusty roads unending.

Knitted Comforts

I express my muffled truths
through Her knitted comforts,
find solitude on moist grass
beneath Her shadow moons,

but Her absence,
Oh, sweet sorrow from salty lips
and nails like icicles,

I find no words but in my sad songs
sung alone by a fire long expired,

like a hell that never came to be
yet a hell continuously begging me:

Unleash me with your fire eye!
Thaw this frozen hell!!

But I sing my songs through knitted socks,
keep the aching feet from freezing,

as I sing my final hymn in joy:
never again to ponder incineration,

Knitted Comforts

I express my muffled truths
through her knitted comforts,
find solitude on moist grass
beneath Her shadow moons,

but Her absence,
Oh, sweet sorrow from salty lips
and nails like icicles,

I find no words but in my sad songs
sung alone by a fire long expired,

like a hell that never came to be
yet a hell continously begging me:

Unleash me with your fire eye!
Thaw this frozen hell!!

But I sing my songs through knitted
                                socks
keep the aching feet from freezing,

as I sing my final hymn in joy:
never again to ponder incineration,

never again to sink much lower
than my soul's divine purpose,
the innate goal of that soul:
to be free – of me.

never again to sink much lower
than my soul's divine purpose,
the innate goal of that soul:
to be free ~ of me.

Tinsel

Snakes in the womb,
in the forge of life;
cold – abandoned
it answers no questions,
no arguments sold
of right or wrong,
of pride or fall.

Worms in the wound,
grim the pace of life;
warm – pulsating,
festering questions
and flawed arguments:
we are masked, betrayed,
tools of a master race;

No! We are merely tinsel,
apparitions shuddering
in cold winter's wind,
riding aimless dreams
along the way
– to meaning.

Tinsel

Snakes in the womb,
in the forge of life;
cold – abandoned
it answers no questions
no arguments sold
of right or wrong
of pride or fall.

Worms in the wound,
grim the pace of life;
warm – pulsating,
festering questions
and flawed arguments:
we are masked, betrayed
tools of a master race;

No! Merely tinsel
apparitions shuddering
in cold winter's wind,
riding purposeless dreams
along the way
– to meaning.

The Sacred Seed

The unbroken chain of myth:
tap, tap, tapping along
to the chorus of your mind,

the perpetuating of the same old truth:
toll, toll, the bell draws you close
to the chorus of their choice,

the silent grave no longer veiled:
with slothlike precision,
a lifetime slowly spooning,
always searching for redemption,
for the sacred seed to the chorus
of a cockroach's final deed.

The Sacred Seed

The unbroken chain of myth:
tap, tap, tapping along
to the chorus of your mind,

the perpetuating of the same old truth:
toll, toll, the bell draws you close
to the chorus of their choice,

the silent grave no longer veiled:
with slothlike precision,
a lifetime slowly spooning,
always searching for redemption
for the sacred seed to the chorus
of a cockroach's final deed,

Dual Moon Madness

Dual moon madness:
I embraced love
only to find her dead;
death became an answer
never sought
yet always portrayed:
pray, be ready
for our lady in red,
be ready
for narrow paths,
be ready
for doors without handle,
be ready
for faceless keyholes.

Hollow dreams
kept me afloat,
awake and aware
of the coming tide,
of the residual madness,
of the missing I
in our final stand;
tender and tethered

Dual Moon Madness

Dual moon madness:
I embraced love
only to find her dead;
death became an answer
never sought
yet always portrayed:
pray, be ready
for our lady in red,
be ready
for narrow paths,
be ready
for doors without handle,
be ready
for faceless key holes.

Hollow dreams
kept me afloat,
awake and aware
of the coming tide,
of the residual madness,
of the missing I
in our final stand;
tender and tethered

I left love behind,
her madness moved mountains
but never moved mine;
my mind set on moving,
to find answers
where the wee lady spoke
of seas without end,
of a golden shore
to set me free
and of an escape
from her deluded dreams
– of a me.

I left love behind,
her madness moved mountains
but never moved mine;
my mind set on moving,
to find answers
where the wee lady spoke
of seas without end,
of a golden shore
to set me free
and of an escape
from her deluded dreams
— of a me.

The C-word

You cringe as you read my words,
my ephemeral expression
diverted from a shattered self
reflecting on the rusty rails beyond:
a disappearing truth
and a tunnel unexplored.

You cringe as you read my words,
my ephemeral expression
diverted to attempt to convey the frail,
the wanted, the tunnel of hope
if only with a single torch
or by Napalm nausea wrought.

You cringe as you read my words,
my ephemeral expression
diverted,
the cracked mirrors of my worlds
and bleach blonde delusions laid bare
without custard, or clotted cream –
or hope.

The C - word

You cringe as you read my words,
my ephemeral expression
diverted from a shattered self
reflecting on the rusty rails beyond:
a disappearing truth
and a tunnel unexplored.

You cringe as you read my words
my ephemeral expression
diverted to attempt to convey the frail,
the wanted, the tunnel of hope
if only with a single torch
or by Napalm nausea wrought,

You cringe as you read my words,
my ephemeral expression
diverted,
the cracked mirrors of my worlds
and bleech blonde delusions laid bare
without custard, or clotted cream –
or hope

Furvus

BAD ROBOT

I blame bad programming,
the programmers themselves
badly programmed
by bad programmers;

I blame bad programming,
the chosen operating system
and low-level language used
by those inherited classes – fools;

I blame bad programmers,
the parental trap of tinkering,
the unspoken words,
and the hereditary misgivings
and real-time environment
unfit for purpose.

Bad Robot

I blame bad programming
the programmers themselves
badly programmed
by bad programmers;

I blame bad programming
the chosen operating system
and low-level language used
by those inherited classes – fools;

I blame bad programmers
the parental trap of tinkering,
the unspoken words,
and the hereditary misgivings
and real-time environment
unfit for purpose.

Friends Lost

Friends lost too early,
untimely departed the long road,
found meandering the lands
of Madness.

Tick – Tock.

From mizzle to drizzle
to the tempest of mind,
no kind of peace were found,
no patience for the patient.

Tick – Tock.

Friends lost too early,
too many too soon
to a Madness roaming
my mind.

Tick – Tock.

Friends lost and none found
on the long and lonely road
out of Madness.

Friends lost

Friends lost too early,
untimely departed the long road,
found meandering the lands
of Madness.

Tick – Tock.

From mizzle to drizzle
to the tempest of mind,
no kind of peace were found,
no patience for the patient.

Tick – Tock.

Friends lost too early,
too many too soon
to a Madness roaming
my mind.

Tick – Tock

Friends lost and none found
on the long and lonely road
out of Madness.

I Remember

I remember, recall and relive
every silent scream sent Your way,
every cold cut of steel received,
every thought of escape perish.

I remember. Yes, I remember

those dreary days of growing,
the instruction manual
unfitting a roadrunner – read
and reread.

I remember. Yes, I remember

the phoney foundations built,
like a yesterday's shivering shower
washing away like a torrent of tears
the last of my lingering hopes.

I remember. Yes, I remember

I remember, I recall and I relive
every silent scream I sent Your way,
every cold cut of steel I received,
every thought of my escape perish.

I remember. Yes, I remember – everything.

I Remember

I remember, recall and relive
every silent scream sent Your way
every cold cut of steel received,
every thought of escape perish.

I remember. Yes, I remember
those dreary days of growing,
the instruction manual
unfitting a roadrunner — read
and reread.

I remember. Yes, I remember
the phoney foundation built,
like yesterdays shivering shower
washing away like a torrent of tears
the last of my lingering hopes.

I remember. Yes, I remember

I remember, I recall and relive
every silent scream I sent Your way,
every cold cut of steel I received,
every thought of my escape perish.

I remember. Yes, I remember — everything

Worried Voices

A voice whispered
of mad … sad … moments
of memory recollection
without trigger,
without purpose:
mindful madness resting
among the stars.

A worried voice had whispered,
in a darkness blacker than black
on a bed of squeaking delight,

Did You Squirt.

A slow *No* had echoed
in the room without a purpose
(bar sleeping and embrace)
now suddenly awake,

>*No, no leaks,*
>*no shattered dreams,*
>*or sore stars sailing far above.*

Then a cold embrace

Worried Voices

A voice whispered
of mad... sad... moments
of memory recollection
without trigger,
without purpose:
mindfull madness resting
among the stars.

A worried voice had whispered
in a darkness blacker than black
on a bed of squeaking delight

Did you squirt.

A slow No had echoed
in the room without purpose
(bar sleeping and embrace)
now suddenly awake.

No, no leaks
no shattered dreams,
or sore stars sailing far above.

Then a cold embrace

in the tenebrous tower,
her farewell and Bon Voyage
produced a ballooning belly
sparked by another's force,
another's life forced upon her.

No ... no leaks ...
no shattered dreams ...

A memory recollected without trigger
and purpose bar reminding
the voice that mindful madness
rests among the stars.

in the tenebrous tower,
her farewell and Bon Voyage
produced a ballooning belly
sparked by another's force,
another's life forced upon her.

No ... no leaks ...
no shattered dreams...

A memory recollected without trigger
and purpose her reminding
the voice that mirdfull madness
rests among the stars.

Long Sleeves Waiting

We joked of *men* coming,
of *men* with purpose,
of *men* bringing white jackets
with extra-long sleeves.

We joked of *men* coming,
of *men* with stern faces,
of *men* in white coats
coming to lock *me* up.

We joked of *men* coming,
of *men* with hateful eyes,
of *men* sent to incarcerate
the one true self.

We joked then, long ago,
voices in unison laughing
at the prospect of *men* coming
of *men* coming for *me*,
for *me*, for
me,

Long Sleeves Waiting

We joked of men coming,
of men with purpose,
of men bringing white jackets
with extra long sleeves.

We joked of men coming,
of men with stern faces,
of men in white coats
coming to lock me up.

We joked of men coming
of men with hateful eyes,
of men sent to incarcerate
the one true self.

We joked then, long ago,
voices in unison laughing
at the prospect of men coming
of men coming for me,
for me, for
me,

We must have joked. . .
but I strangled your mirth
battered it into silence,
my mindful scar a reminder
as I wear my final frock,
on this day of days
the gods' chosen outfit:
a gleaming white jacket
with extra-long sleeves.

Furvus

We must have joked...
but I strangled your mirth
battered it into silence,
my mindfull scar a reminder
as I wear my final frock
on this day of days
the gods' chosen outfit:
a gleaming white jacket
with extra long sleeves.

The Halls of the Dead

Beyond my breaking belief an abode,
the bell every hour on the hour
summons the Dead and the Dreary,
the Worried and the Weary;
a branch off a master trunk
old as the dusty dreams
said to be the only truth
worth clinging to.

Beneath a dust cover high above
rattling remains of one who spoke
at length and at depth at everyone
and everything congregated;
now silence fills the void
left to those still present:
the Dead and the Dreary,
the Worried and the Weary,
in an abode far beyond
my fascination.

The Halls of the Dead

Beyond my breaking belief an abode,
the bell every hour on the hour
summons the Dead and the Dreary,
the Worried and the Weary;
a branch of a master trunk
old as the dusty dreams
said to be the only truth
worth clinging to.

Beneath a dust cover high above
rattling remains of one who spoke
at length and at depth at everyone
and everything congregated;
now silence fills the void
left to those still present:
the Dead and the Dreary,
the Worried and the Weary,
in an abode far beyond
my fascination.

Forever Fallout

I woke one morning to find the bear awake
when winter storms should have kept him
safely asleep.

As I woke in a sweat with a lingering dread
a sound echoed deep within:
there was to be a third war of men,
another war to end all ends,

with cowards hiding deep within their dolls
of past triumphs, and a railway across the land
once permanently frozen carrying little yellow men
in aid of the faltering knights of pale.

I woke one morning to the briefest of news,
I am yet to resume my life knowing death
now walks among us; as sure as sure can be,
no one will be spared as the firework starts
and the forever fallout
– spreads.

forever
fallout

Hayden Veil

A Waltz for One

I dance an unwelcome waltz
with daemons bent on purging
all that once was my life,
now merely fading memories
among their dust thrown up.

I hoover and I sweep their hell
from the sanded floors far below,
my shadows flicker
as the tapers embrace
an unworthy life.

I paint their town in colours,
the black and the greys, colours
befitting the foul and rogue rascals
you once called out in passing.

I wash my hand of all their sins,
betraying the betrayed
as the only way out,

the only way out
– of destitution.

A Waltz for One

I dance an unwelcome waltz
with demons bent on purging
all that once was my life,
now merely fading memories
among their dust thrown up.

I hoover and I sweep their hell
from the sanded floor far below,
my shadows flicker
as the tapers embrace
an unworthy life.

I paint their town in colours,
the black and the greys, colours
befitting the foul and rogue rascals
you once called out in passing.

I wash my hands of all their sins,
betraying the betrayed
as the only way out,

the only way out
— of destitution

DEATH

Death is my final poem,
I will write till the ink runs out,
I will write the wordless eulogy:
of days of night,
of the raven's flight,
of the nomad,
the no-man – spoiled.

Death is my final poem,
I will croon if only I could
exclude tribulations, as tributes
like a springless river or a fountain
of youthful dreams – run dry.

Death is my final poem,
I will mourn the empty parchments,
I will mourn their absence,
I will mourn in silent contemplation.

Death is my final poem.
The dawning of the frozen time;
the unticking clock of awakening;
the primary cycle interrupted.

Hark! He knocks.

Death

Death is my final poem,
I will write till the ink runs out,
I will write the wordless eulogy:
of days of night,
of the raven's flight,
of the nomad,
the no-man — spoiled.

Death is my final poem,
I will croon if only I could
exclude tribulations, as tributes
like a springless river or a fountain
of youthful dreams — run dry.

Death is my final poem,
I will mourn the empty parchments,
I will mourn their absence,
I will mourn in silent contemplation.

Death is my final poem.
The drawing of the frozen time;
the unticking clock of awakening;
the primary cycle interrupted.

Hark! He knocks.

Death is my final poem.
Unwritten by shaking hands,
by eyes weakened and the grey tears
of a heaven.

Hark! Again the pounding.

Death is my final poem.
Distractions of deluded grandeur
sail above innocent clouds.

Hark! Hark!

Death is my final poem.
Dissonance from unread mail, and drawers
of dull knives calling.

Hark?

Death is the final poem
I will write

... as I unlock all possible futures
making every road mine ...

Death is my final poem.
Unwritten by shaking hands,
by eyes weakened and the grey beats
of a heaven.

Hark! Again the pounding.

Death is my final poem.
Distractions of deluded grandeur
sail above innocent clouds.

Hark! Hark!

Death is my final poem.
Dissonance from unread mail, and
                              drawers
of dull knives calling.

Hark?

Death is the final poem
I will write

...as I unlock all possible futures
    making every road mine...

There is no truth
— Only stories

NOTES

1. as, to be honest, nobody else will ever read this book!
2. *shakes his head in disbelief*. Poet? As if … as if

About the Author

In an earlier incarnation, Hayden Veil enjoyed a successful career in software engineering, writing late-night poetry in pursuit of sanity.

On 2 February 2020, the world of Hayden Veil changed: *Ghosts* became real and with its soul laid bare there was no turning back from the perpetual path of poetry.

The adventure continued with *Imbalance* in 2021. An attempt to further explore the composition of a poetry collection by incorporating graphics to accompany the poetry.